The Dash
Making Sure Your Obituary Won't Suck

Tom Morrison

WALDORF PUBLISHING

Published by Waldorf Publishing
2140 Hall Johnson Road
#102-345
Grapevine, Texas 76051
www.WaldorfPublishing.com

The Dash
Making Sure Your Obituary
Won't Suck

ISBN: 978-1-64136-973-2
Library of Congress Control Number: 2018933207

Copyright © 2018

FOREWARD

I know what you're thinking. Who the heck is Eric Szymanski, and why did I turn to this page instead of going straight to the first chapter of Tom's book? I'll do my best to make this worth your time.

As I write this, I'm so "Naked and Afraid". I helped Tom write the title of this book, and now he wants me to write the Foreword. What the heck is a Foreword, anyway? This is "*SO, Tom Morrison*!" He is getting me to do something I've never done before in front of an intimate audience. He loves to get people out of their comfort zone. But who am I kidding? I am not a writer...I work in Sales. Where is the last time I heard that? Oh yeah, I remember...

The last time I heard the words, "You just don't understand, you work in Sales" was when I was surrounded by four (yes, four) large bouncers while hosting Tom and his wife, DeAnna, at a two-day VIP Client Showcase at a world-famous tourist destination. The bouncers were there to escort me (*ME, not Tom*), out of the establishment. Mind you, I was *the Host* – and the bar was at MY Resort. I'm getting bounced out of a club, at a bar that I represent, in front of a client. What the hell? I even have the word *Senior* in my job title. I'm having an out of body experience, I'm wondering why I'm explaining myself to the "brute squad" and hoping I don't get fired. Meanwhile, Tom has worked his way inside, enjoying his drink and conversation. This is just like Tom. How in the world could this be happening? I'll try to explain...

It's 1:27 am and we just finished cocktails and dancing at a night club after party...aka "Networking" in Tom's language. We're in a boardwalk setting and we're walking to the valet area to procure a ride back to our resort. The night is over…or so I thought. As we were walking, Tom hears more music coming from another bar. He wants to go in for a second afterglow. A second afterglow?! Did I mention it's 1:27 am? Who does that? Oh yeah…Tom does. Why? Because Tom wants to make sure his obituary won't suck. His favorite hashtag is #LiveInTheMoment. It's all about memorable experiences for Tom, while dragging his friends along for the ride. So, Tom turns to me and says, "I forgot my lanyard (i.e. event name badge) in the previous club." I felt it was my responsibility to ensure that Tom had his name badge at our event the next day. With both clubs closing in less than 3 minutes, I had to act fast. I tell Tom to go inside bar #2 and order a round of drinks. I will go back to the club #1 to retrieve his lanyard. Time is of the essence. With me wearing professional attire, but no name tag or company credentials, I quickly state to the bouncer in bar #2 that I'm a leader at the company. I'm hosting clients for a 2-day VIP tour, and I'm heading over to retrieve something from club #1 (which is next door) and will be right back. Tom had told me exactly where it was. The plan is set. Tom and DeAnna walk in to bar #2 while I walk back to the club #1 to retrieve Tom's lanyard. I make record time. Tom's lanyard is exactly where he said it would be. I'll bet I was gone maybe 60 seconds from the door of bar #2. When I return to join Tom, the door is closed. I check my watch, it's 1:29am. I pull the door handle and *it's locked.* Are you kidding me, there is still one-minute left!

My clients are inside. I'm standing outside the locked door, holding Tom's lanyard like a game show contestant with a parting gift. What am I going to do? I told my client to go inside and everything would be ok. What if it's not? It's my responsibility to ensure they are safe. Just breathe… Take a moment and think. The bouncer's watch must have been a little fast. He must have closed and locked the door so other guests could not go inside. I'm sure he wouldn't mind if I walked to the back door and went inside, right? After all, I explained the situation. We both work there, it will all be ok, right? I was so wrong. I walk past several employees as I stroll through the back door. I wave, smile, and make eye contact. I have nothing to hide, I'm a "Senior Manager." I enter the establishment. Tom and DeAnna have already ordered another round of drinks. I walk over, hand Tom his lanyard, and exhale as I believe the crisis has been averted. Little did I know, that while solving Tom's lanyard crisis, I had created my own personal invitation to "Bouncer Wonderland".

I'm sitting down with Tom and DeAnna, when four large men walk over to me and ask me to leave…immediately. They can't be serious. I try to explain the situation. I'm hosting clients. I'm a leader at the company. I spoke with the bouncer at the door. It's right at that moment I realize that one of the four bouncers *was* the bouncer from the front door. They are not backing down. My words are going unheard. They do not want to talk this over. What am I going to do? There is no reference to this in the employee handbook. I had a choice – escalate or diffuse the situation. I chose to try to diffuse the situation. I tell Tom and DeAnna, "Please stay here and finish your drink. I'll walk to the back office and talk to the bouncers and the bar manager. We'll work this out. It's a simple misunderstanding."

Tom, DeAnna, and the "four horsemen" all agree to this plan. Excellent! I'm escorted to the back office. Three brutes stay with me, while one goes to find the manager. Long story short, they don't care who I am, or what I'm doing here. By the way, the first words out of my mouth is that Tom is the CEO of an organization who can fill the bar with patrons.

This is very embarrassing for them (not me). I'm here to demonstrate the good time you could have at the bar, so Tom will return with hundreds of his members. They are ruining it. The manager comes over. I repeat my story and ask if he wants to call my boss at 1:40 am to confirm who I am, not knowing if they would answer the call.

My story was met with a unified response – "you must leave now." That's when it came out of the original bouncer... *"You just don't understand, you work in Sales! You think you can do whatever you want."* It was at a that moment that I realized we were at a stalemate. ...but I knew something they didn't know... While we were in the back office, I was giving Tom and DeAnna time to finish their drinks. I was stalling the manager and the bouncers to give my clients the time they needed. I apologized to the "walking muscle trees" and offered to leave with my clients immediately. They said that's all they wanted in the first place. Mission accomplished! I walked back into the bar and Tom asked if everything was ok. I observed their glasses were nearly empty and asked if they were ready to leave. Thankfully, Tom said, "yes," and we were out of there like a bat out of hell.

The next morning, I arrived at our event. The first thing I said to the nearest senior leader is, "I think I may be fired today." I explained what happened, and she said everything would be ok. It turns out that our company did *not* manage that particular bar, so *technically* I *was* trespassing. Oh, Snap! Rest assured! I lived to sell another day!

Let me remind you that the only reason I almost lost my job due to trespassing was because Tom wanted to go to a "second afterglow" at 1:27 am to create another awesome life memory...without his freaking name badge. Soon afterwards, Tom signed a contract with my company to host his conference at our establishment. He never confirmed this, but I'm pretty sure one of the main reasons Tom chose our company was because I demonstrated my willingness to lose my job to make sure he could have a good time with his wife…while I almost got beat up by four very large men.

Many would have called it a night at 1:27 am that night…not Tom. He has a passion for life, and a "live in the moment" attitude to create a balance and quality of life that people admire and desire. He wants the same for you.

My question is, "Are you living the quality of life you really, really want? …or do you feel like you are just going through the motions in life?" If you disappeared, would anyone care? Do you ever feel the mountain is too steep to climb, or you don't have enough time to get it all done? Maybe you have some success, but you don't know how to get to the next level.

If you already have the perfect life, this book may not be for you. Put the book down, and step away from the table. Take a moment or two and congratulate yourself on your awesomeness. You have arrived!

If your life isn't perfect and you're still reading this, congratulations. Try not to feel bad about your less than perfect situation. I'm right there with you. You are not alone. We've all been there, and this too shall pass.

You may be wondering, "how do I get from where I am now to where I want to be?" There must be something I can do. There is…

The knowledge you will gain from reading Tom's book is the path for discovering your desires, chasing your dreams, and living a life so your obituary won't suck. Don't stop here. Turn the page to chapter one, keep reading, and start creating the life you want today!

Eric Szymanski
No-Nonsense Hospitality Professional
Association Industry Professional
Member of Tom's Wolfpack
Survivor of Tom's Bachelor Party
Attendee and M.C. of Tom & DeAnna's Wedding
Barbershop Quartet Singer
Husband & Father

Eric's Dash-

Eric was born and raised in the suburbs of Detroit, Michigan, where he was a member of the East Middle School 8th Grade Football Team. Eric played Offense and Defense on this team, which was undefeated and unscored upon. His mother did not let him continue his dream to play high school football though…he played in the freaking Marching Band, and watched his teammates win the State Football Championship…

Table Of Contents

CHAPTER 1

BETWEEN THE NUMBERS

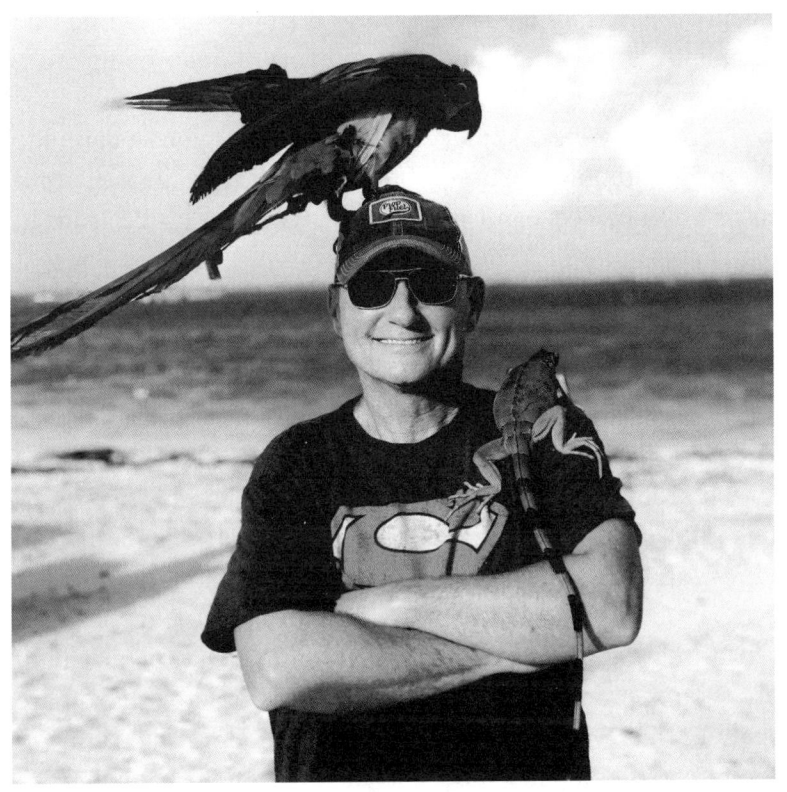

As you stare at the dash of someone's life, you stare into their joy, success, hurt, and pain.

What will your dash represent?

If you were to count the world's population, there would be over 7,500,000,000 people on earth. That's right. A lot of zeros, which means a bunch of people. Now if you were to try and find one commonality among 100% of the world's population, it would be virtually impossible. Everyone has some individual trait that separates the population into smaller groups such as nationality, gender, age, ethnicity, or occupation to name a few. It really is impossible to find one element that is a common link to every human being…except for one…the Dash.

You may be asking, "Tom, what do you mean, the Dash?" Without question, 100% of all people in the world have a Dash. You can't get rid of it. You can't hide from it. You can't ignore it. You can't run from it. You can't throw it away. When each person is born, they are born with a Dash. Your Dash is the small hyphen that separates two numbers over your lifetime. The number to the left of your Dash is the start of your life. The number on the right of your Dash is the end of your life. The Dash in the middle is your life.

It seems like only a simple line that separates two numbers, but in reality, it represents EVERYTHING about you. How you lived your life, what people think about you, what you stood for, and the legacy you will be remembered for. All of the happiness, joy, success, failure, victory, and pain are wrapped up inside of your Dash. It's obvious if you are reading this book, you don't have a number on the right, so read on and take close notes. Your life is about to change.

The question for you is how is your dash playing out? Are you experiencing the quality of life you dreamed of as a young person? Are you checking off your bucket list now, or are you waiting until retirement? Are you building memories with those you love most? Are you saying what you would like to say to someone now instead of waiting until it's too late? Are you building the memories doing what you REALLY want to do in life? The biggest question of all is, "As you think about how your Dash is playing out, will your obituary suck?"

At the end of everyone's life, their Dash is translated in their obituary. The world will get to read how you lived your life, what you stood for, and what your legacy is about, in your obituary. For me, in that moment of people reading what makes up my Dash, I don't want my obituary to suck. I want people to see that I lived my dreams, chased incredible experiences I loved, and cared for those closest to me. Most people want these same three elements of chasing their dreams, creating great memories, and to be loved in their life. Most people, however, don't. I could fill this book with an entire set of excuses as to why they don't pursue the best life possible, but I'm not about excuses. I'm about you, your hope, your dreams, and you living the best life possible. I want that for you.

Do you want more from your life? Do you have dreams you would like to chase? Do you have people you would like to have a better relationship with? Do you have life goals that you would love to achieve? Do you have adventures you would like to take? If you desire to live the best life possible and live a quality of life that is fulfilling to your soul each day, you are in the right place.

As I speak around the country on generational differences, many Baby Boomers feel that the younger generation wants to play too much instead of work. I feel that many in the Baby Boomer generation fault the Millennials for their desire to have a nice work/life balance at such a young age. Baby Boomers were taught to work, work, work, from youth to retirement, and then you retire and enjoy life. The problem is that most Boomers woke up in their early 50s, wondering where the time went, looking for meaning in their life, and wondering why they were waiting on retirement to begin enjoying life. Many called it the "mid-life crisis." I think boomers just rediscovered their life at 50 and now want to start living it again.

Many in the younger generation got to watch that work, work, work quality of life plays out in their parents' lives, and what did many see in their parents? Debt, divorce, stress, and unfilled dreams over a lifetime. Young people watched their parents live lives that lead to wondering in their 50s, where did all the time go? Why didn't I live life more? Society should not fault the younger generation for their refreshing philosophy of work/life balance. We should embrace it.

A long life is no guarantee. We should all be living life every day, in a way that brings us joy, smiles, happiness, and fulfillment. That doesn't mean that every day will be perfect, but in those imperfect days, you will at least be living a quality of life that you want. No matter what age you are, I want you to chase your dreams, experience your bucket list, and live life in a way that every day makes you smile and say, "MY LIFE ROCKS!"

To help give you some focus and motivation to chase the experiences and quality of life that you really desire, let's do a little life assessment. The following is a picture with 78 squares in it. These squares represent the average life span of a person living in the United States. I want you to take a pencil or pen, and color in the number of squares that represent your age. For example, if you are 56, color in 56 squares.

Life Block Exercise

Color in the number of squares of your age

Those not colored is what you have left to live

Once you have colored in the squares, I want you to stare at that picture and realize that the colored portion is what you have lived in life. The white squares are what you have left to live. This is a general visual of the time-line of your Dash.

Some questions I want to ask you at this point as you stare at this image:

- Are you satisfied with what you have done so far?
- Do your decisions align with where you would really like to be in life?
- Are there people you need to forgive to experience emotional freedom?
- Are there people you need to ask forgiveness from for your actions?
- Does your soul feel fulfilled at this very moment?
- How would the closest people to you describe you to others if you weren't around?
- Are there things stored up in your heart that you need to say to your parents, children, spouse, or friends?
- What is on your bucket list?
- What are you going to do with the time you have left?

As you think of those questions, let me add something to the equation: what happens when tragedy strikes, or you go to the doctor and receive a diagnosis that instantly colors in almost all of your blocks? Don't say it won't happen to you…it happens every single day, to people everywhere, of all ages. Every day people young and old are diagnosed with cancer, have an unexpected heart attack, or are involved in a serious accident. In that moment when anyone finds themselves in the back of an ambulance or in a hospital bed, life becomes real…and so does the number on the right side of your Dash. You wish you had done more. You wish you had forgiven someone. You wish you had said some things to those closest to you. You wish you had taken that trip. You wish you had… The list goes on and on.

With that in mind, I want to encourage you to have a "live-in-the-moment attitude each day." I want you to be open to experiencing life, adventure, and to get outside of your comfort zone, by doing things that you want to do, but are always claiming no time or money to do. There is no time like today to experience life! No longer live with the attitude, "I'll have tomorrow", or "I'll do it next year."

There were two people I knew closely that I want to tell you about that will bring the, "live in the moment" point home. The first person I would like to tell you about is Chelsea. She was the daughter of my cousin. A beautiful, bubbly 19-year-old, who always brought a smile to anyone around her. She had married her sweetheart at 19, and soon after became pregnant with their first child. They lived a great life as a young couple, enjoying a tight bond with their family and friends. She woke up on her 19th birthday thinking that day was going to be a glorious day, which it was. She had an amazing husband, was two months away from having her first child, and was going to celebrate her big day with her family.

I can remember the back-to-back Facebook posts like it was yesterday. Chelsea posted right before going to bed on her birthday night how awesome the day was; how amazing her family was. The very next post was her mother's post the next morning asking for everyone to pray for Chelsea. You see, Chelsea woke up the next morning after her incredible 19th birthday, had an aneurism, and fell into a coma. She lasted in that coma in the hospital until her little baby boy was born with no complications. A month later, Chelsea was no longer with us here on earth.

What I would like to share about Chelsea is that in the few months she lived in a coma, she reached more hearts, and changed more lives than most people impact in a lifetime. It was very inspiring to experience seeing people's lives changing amidst Chelsea's tragedy.

The second person I want you to take note of is Ray Kroc, the founder of McDonalds. Many people don't know it, but Ray Kroc discovered McDonalds in his fifties. Yes, in his fifties. Can you believe that? While most people would have given up on their dreams, Ray Kroc discovered that it's never too late to chase your dreams. Over the years, McDonalds has become a huge success in the fast food industry.

Here is what I want you to take away from these two real-life stories:

- We are not promised tomorrow…don't live like it.
- It's never too late to chase your dreams; start today.

My motto in life is, "If I'm asked to go on an adventure, journey, or experience of any kind, and I have the time and money, I say "YES" …every time." My favorite saying is, "I'm IN!" The reason why? It's simple…I don't want my obituary to suck. I want my obituary to be representative of a person who lived life in a way that fulfilled my dreams, brought daily joy, and ignited passion.

This simple philosophy has helped me, "live in the moment" throughout my entire life and create life memories that cause me to smile and laugh at constantly. It doesn't matter whether it's dinner, going to the movie, taking a snow skiing trip, or any other life experience…if I'm invited and I have the time and money, I'M IN!

"Live in the moment" and "I'm IN" are the two phrases that are your commitment to making sure that your obituary won't suck. I want to encourage you to embrace these two phrases as you read this book.

Don't be someone who "wished they had." Be an "I did" person. Start today being a person who seizes every day as if you only had one block left to fulfill your dreams in the block exercise. Be the person who writes their bucket list down and pursues it. Be the person who sees people as human beings who need help and be there to help. Be the person who writes their career goals down and accomplishes them. Be the person who decides what you want your legacy to be and makes it happen.

Many reading this book are saying, "Tom, I don't want my obituary to suck. I want to be an 'I'm IN' person. I just don't know how or where to start."

My friend, this is your lucky day, because that is what this book is all about!

CHAPTER 2

BE THE CEO OF YOUR DASH

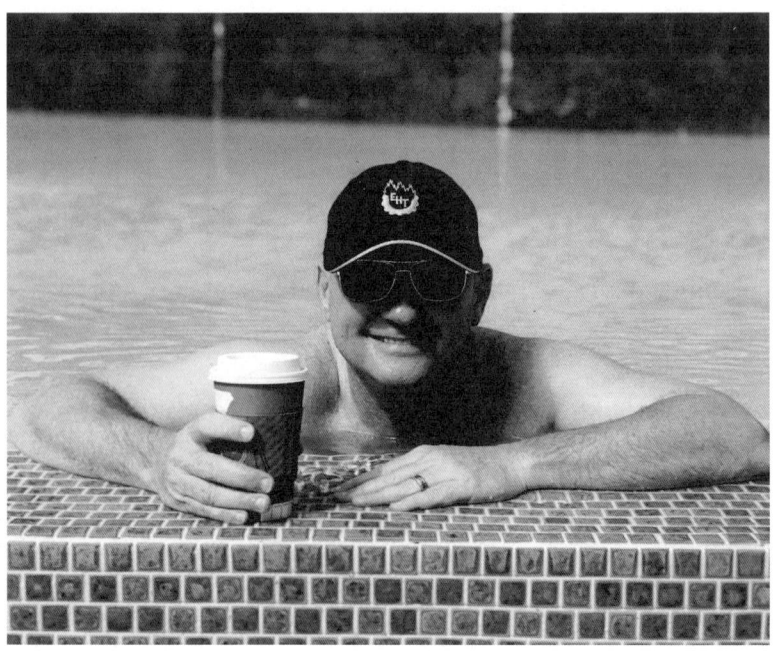

*"Things are never as bad as you think, you have more
control over your life than you think, and you have
more influence on your circumstances than you think."*

When it comes to life, I want to dispel something that
many people have never been taught throughout their life.
It is the frustration of many young people, and many adults
don't want to believe it: THERE ARE WINNERS, AND
THERE ARE LOSERS IN LIFE. Now, I don't mean that
people are characterized as winners and losers, allow me
to explain... In the results of life events, there are winners,
and there are losers. When you are out in the real world,
everyone is not as good as everyone else, and not everyone

gets a trophy. In the world, out of ten people in an interview, only one gets hired and nine do not. One person won the interview and nine lost. When there are ten proposals for a business deal, one wins and nine lose. If you are to live life without frustration, it is crucial that you understand that you are going to be on the losing end in some circumstances. The question is, "What do you do with that moment of losing?" You can have a pity party and be frustrated that the world isn't fair, or you can learn from those losses and choose to use it to improve yourself, so you become stronger, better, and more positive. My point is, life isn't an even playing field. It is highly competitive; you must work hard, work to earn it, and be dedicated to achieving your goals. Even when you give 100% of yourself in the process, you are going to lose a time or two, but if you give 100%, you will not lose nearly as much as those who aren't willing to even do what it takes to achieve their goals. Two key things to live by in life are: learn how to accept loss with class and grace and hate to lose more than you like to win. This mindset will help you to not let losing devastate your life, but instead, drive you to continue giving your all in the process.

So many people walk through their life with so much anxiety and fear, all because their life feels so out of their control. They are worrying about all the things that they feel they can't control, yet they are forgetting to get their hands on the things that they can control...and do those things incredibly well. You need to understand that you are the CEO of your own life. When I say "CEO", I mean the Chief Energy Officer. The buck stops with you. No one can hurt your feelings if you don't give them control of your feelings. No one can control your life long term if you don't allow them to. No one can make you do things against your beliefs, unless you let them. If you are allowing people or circumstances to control you, then you need to find the strength and a path to take back control of your life and become the CEO of your own life. This book is about rediscovering yourself as CEO and living the quality of life you desire…so your obituary won't suck. Do not give anyone who doesn't deserve it, the editorial rights of your obituary.

There is a saying I heard one time in a business seminar, which really is one of the key central points to you making your life count, and fulfilling all of the dreams you desire, "You get what you tolerate, or you get what you demand." Throughout your life, your circumstances, your job, your family, and sometimes even the people closest to you, will bring things your way that will have a negative impact on your life. So many overlook those things by saying:

- "They didn't really mean that."
- "If you would just get to know them, you would like them."
- "It's just a phase, they will come out of it one day."
- "I know they wouldn't do anything to hurt me."
- "I know they will pay me back."

I'm here to tell you, that if you allow anyone to take advantage of you, sometimes even people who you never thought would do such a thing, will take advantage of you. I've seen it happen between friends, immediate family members, and even in employer/employee relationships. If you are going to obtain the quality of life that you really want, that is stress and anxiety free, it is imperative that you decide what you will, and what you will not tolerate from people. You need to draw those lines and stick to them. When people see that you are serious about those lines, they don't cross them. If they do, you kindly and respectfully let them know that if they can't change their behavior, you won't actively associate with them until they do. This goes for even close family members. If they truly care about you, they will adjust their behavior to one of care and respect.

Just so you can see some examples of those lines, here are a few of mine:

- Don't ask me to put my work before my family.
- You will treat me with decency as a human being.
- Children are never allowed to disrespect or directly disobey.
- Being a hard worker isn't defined by making me work 50+ hours every week.
- Just because you are family, doesn't mean that you can treat me with disrespect.
- If you can't find anything good to say, don't say it to me.
- When we are in a restaurant, you will not run around like you are on an outdoor playground.
- Don't bring drama without facts and a solution.

These are just a few of the numerous agreements that I have made with myself with regards to certain behaviors that I will not tolerate. These are the lines that keep a positive balance on your life and make it stress free. Stress comes from allowing these chaotic behaviors to exist in your life. Some of these may be the same as yours, and you may have others as well. The key thing is to write these down and decide not to tolerate these behaviors, but rather to demand that people around you adhere to them.

A lot of people probably look at a few of them and think, "I was a tyrant and overly rigid with my children." If you were to interview both of my kids, you would hear from them that I was one of the most fun, caring fathers you would ever meet. They would also tell you that I was a good disciplinarian as well and helped them understand what "boundaries" and "consequences" meant in life. I worked diligently to make sure my kids knew where the lines were drawn between good behavior and bad behavior...respect and disrespect, and what consequences would be from certain behaviors. I taught them that if your actions make other's lives unnecessarily more difficult, don't EXPECT anything good in return. The easier, and more anxiety-free you make other people's lives, the more they will want to experience life with you.

Daily life for most is a grind, and people have enough negative forces pulling at their life. If you inflict unnecessary conflict into it, they will almost always say "no" to your requests or will not want to be around you very much. If you want your obituary to not suck, it is important to have people in your life...the right people who enrich your life. We will dig more into people later on.

Now, many of you who have changed your mind over the years from, "I want people to respect me," to "I want people to like me," are going to have a tough road ahead. People who want others to respect them, are willing to walk away from people who cross the lines that they have agreed they will not tolerate. People who want to "be liked by everyone" chase after people who are crossing their lines, simply because they feel there is something wrong with themselves. Hear this: There is nothing wrong with you! In a lot of cases, the reason the other person isn't creating a positive environment in your life, has more to do with them and their insecurities than it does with you. They are dealing with their own past and stuff in their life, and it is playing itself out against you. There is nothing you can do to fix that. Now, does that mean you ignore them for the rest of your life? No, it simply means you let them know you will not tolerate certain behaviors that cross your lines of respect, human decency, and emotional bullying.

The bottom line is that people have a higher level of respect for you if you have drawn some basic, good, and accepted behavioral standards for your life, and expect them to treat you within those standards. Decide what you will not tolerate and put them in your mobile device, so you have them at your fingertips for reference. It's so easy to forget our principles sometimes in the emotions of life. Removing the negative people in your life will definitely increase the odds that your obituary will not suck.

CHAPTER 3

YOUR PERSONAL GDP

*"On a scale of 1 to 10, who wants to live a 6.8 life?
The difference between a 6.8 and a 10 quality of life are
goals, discipline, and persistence."*

Now I want to get into what I feel is the most essential
two elements of this entire book. These two elements are the
essential cornerstones for how to make sure your obituary
won't suck. They are:

- Personal GDP Rating

- The Path to the Ultimate Life Visual

First, I want to talk about your Personal GDP Rating. Your Personal GDP Rating is the average rating of yourself in 12 key areas of life on a scale of 1 to 10 (1 being, I NEED HELP, and 10 being, MY LIFE IS AWESOME). Of course, we all know a perfect 10 is impossible, because at least one of the 12 key areas will be under a 10 and needing some attention. Let's break down the 12 key areas of your Personal GDP.

Just like the economy has a GDP, or Gross Domestic Product that tells us how well the economy is growing or declining, your own Personal GDP Rating tells you how you feel that your overall life is playing out on a scale from one to ten. The following is how each element of GDP is defined:

G stands for GOALS. As I said earlier, you will not maximize your life experiences and the quality of your life if you don't have goals in the areas of:

- Finances
- Health
- Career
- Relationships

I encourage people to have at least one achievable goal in each area, every year. Studies show that 90% of the time, people who have goals achieve at a higher level than those who don't. Goals lay the path of where you want to go. If you don't know where you are going, you never have a benchmark to know if you are making any progress in your life. Goals are essential if you are to raise your quality of life, and we will discuss them more in depth in chapter 14.

D stands for DISCIPLINE. Discipline is those daily habits that you execute that build on one another to ensure that you reach your goals. Whether you want a high GPA in school, to reach a certain salary level, retire by a certain date, or buy a new home, you must have daily, disciplined behavior that will get you to your goals. Your daily disciplines must align with the goals you set for yourself. If you want to have a high GPA, you need study discipline. If you want to buy a house, you need saving money discipline. If you want to retire, you must have investing discipline. If you want to lose weight, you need diet and workout disciplines. You see, you must connect the right disciplines to achieve the desired goal. Building a consistent set of disciplined habits ensures that you stay on target to meeting your goals each year.

With the area of Discipline, there are four factors that control 99% of your success in any goal. They are:
- Choices You Make
- How You Spend Your Money
- How You Invest Your Time
- The People You Surround Yourself With

It doesn't matter what your goal is, if you aren't on the road to reaching it, one or more of these Disciplines are not in alignment with your goal and needs to be looked at. It is important that you are looking at your goals on a quarterly basis and analyzing:
- Where you are in meeting your goals.
- Where should you be at that moment in time.
- Steps to make up the gaps in where you should be and where you actually are.

If you do this every quarter and are serious about making any changes needed to achieve your goals, then you will be successful in creating the life you desire.

P stands for PERSISTENCE. In life, so many people came up just short of success because they weren't persistent for long enough to reach their goal. They gave up. They quit. They didn't want it bad enough. Life isn't easy and many goals you set aren't going to just happen. It is going to take hard work and working smart to make it happen. Four characteristics I believe are critical for everyone to have to execute their daily disciplines for success are:

- Ability to Adapt
- Positive Attitude
- Good Communication Skills
- Perseverance

Now that we have briefly outlined each of the elements of your Personal GDP Rating, here is an example of how you perform your own rating. Every quarter rate yourself on a scale from 1 to 10 (1 being, "I need help in this area"; 5 being, "I'm doing average"; and 10 being, "this area of my life is awesome"). Once you have all 12 areas rated, you add them up and divide by 12. This will give you your Personal GDP Rating at that moment in time. You can also go to my website and download my Excel spreadsheet that will allow you to enter your ratings on a quarterly basis, and it automatically calculates your Personal GDP Rating. I recommend downloading the form and using it, so you can easily track your progress. To download the rating form, go to TomMorrison.biz and click on the Personal GDP Rating form under the "Tom's Book" tab across the top.

The following is an example of how to do your own Personal GDP Rating:

AREA	RATING
• Finances	6.3
• Career / Business	7.4
• Relationships	8.6
• Health	8.0
• Choices You Make	7.2
• How You Spend Your Money	7.0

- How You Invest Your Time   6.9
- The People You Surround Yourself With   8.0
- Ability to Adapt   6.0
- Positive Attitude   6.0
- Good Communication Skills   7.5
- Perseverance   6.8

PERSONAL GDP RATING: **7.14**

In the example above, this person rating themselves had an overall rating of 7.14. The big question is, "Are you satisfied living a 7.14 life?" I don't believe a 10.0 life is possible, simply because there is always some area of life that can be improved. I believe it's even tough to have a 9.0 life, but I do believe an 8.5 life is accomplishable. For me, if you are living an 8.5 life, you have everything in your life moving in the right direction, and you are on the way to meeting your goals and accomplishing the life you want. The good news is that once you have done your rating, you can clearly see the areas that you need to improve on, then work toward getting your life on the right path towards meeting your goals and reaching your dreams.

If you look at the example rating on the previous page, you can immediately see that this person needs to look at the following areas for improvement to their Personal GDP Rating and how they feel about their life:

- Finances
- Time Management
- Ability to Adapt
- Perseverance
- Attitude

In each of these areas, they scored themselves below a

7.0. These are the initial focus areas that this person would want to make improvements to over the next quarter.

Now let's dig into the *Path to the Ultimate Life* visual that I spoke of earlier. This visual brings to light the keys as to why your life is where it is today, and the keys to how you can make change to maximize the experiences in your Dash.

In my opinion, for anyone to live the best life possible, you must have an annual goal for four key areas of your life:

- Finances
- Career / Business
- Relationships
- Health

Everyone's quality of life is driven by what happens in these four key areas. If you have no goals, you don't know where you are going, have no basis to see progress, and will run off on unnecessary "rabbit trails" in life. You need a goal in each area to ensure that you stay focused on the path to the life you desire.

As you wake up each day, you make choices that either create and open opportunities in each of these areas, or close and limit opportunities in your life. You are in control of these choices, so it is important that you understand the influences that control the path you take in chasing your dreams and the quality of life you really want.

The following visual I designed has eight dynamic elements that you need to excel at in order to accomplish your goals and live the life you desire. I have mentioned each of these in the discussion of performing your Personal GDP Rating.

It is important to gain a keen understanding of these 8 elements. They will each play a crucial role in you making sure your obituary won't suck, and in you maximizing your experiences between the numbers.

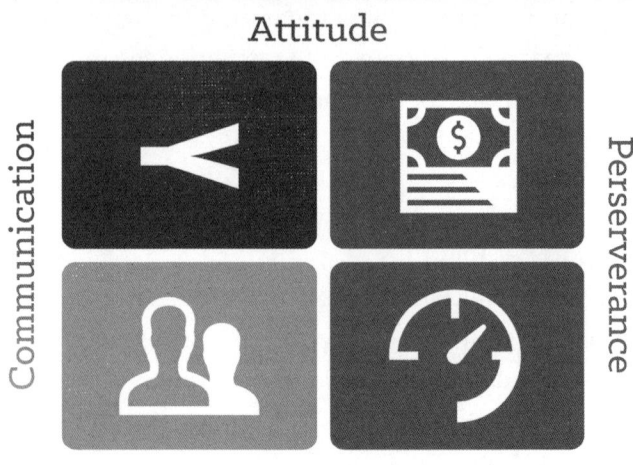

The ***Path to the Ultimate Life*** visual has four blocks on the inside, I will call "Pillars," and four words on the outside, I call "Characteristics." The Pillars on the inside are the four things that have the most impact on your life every day and are the things you MUST do well to obtain the life you want. They are:

- Choices
- Money
- Time
- People

The four words on the outside are the four Characteristics that you MUST possess to do the four Pillars with excellence. Those are:

- Attitude
- Ability to Adapt

- Communication
- Perseverance

I contend that if your life is not going the way you want, or if you are not getting the fulfillment out of life that you want, one of the four Pillars are out of alignment in your life. Either, you're not making good choices, you aren't spending your money wisely, you're not investing your time soundly, you are not surrounded by the right people, or you are struggling with one or more of the four characteristics.

Let's take a look at each of the four Pillars and Characteristics and put them in context so you know why they are all so important and inter-connected.

CHOICES

The sideways "Y" in the top right corner box of Pillars represents the fork in the road you come to on a daily basis. Every day you make choices. They are either good or bad choices and warrant good or bad consequences in your life. As you continue down a road of bad choices, they tend to multiply and make things worse. Learning how to make good choices is a mindset of how to analyze what is good for your life and what isn't. I know many people who want to earn $100,000 a year, but aren't willing to make the good choice to go to college, or at least a two-year technical school to find a high paying trade to work in. I know others who want to own a business but aren't willing to make the serious set of decisions needed for owning a company. They just want it handed to them. I know high school students who want to go to a good university but aren't making the right choices to keep their GPA at a level that gets them accepted. Remember, your choices dictate your lifestyle. Make bad choices, your life will be very frustrating. Make good choices, and your life will progress towards the life you really want.

One last thing I will say on choices, is that if you do not like where you are in life…you don't like the neighborhood you live in…you don't like the weight you are at…you don't like your job, or you just don't like your circumstances, you are always just one decision and three action steps away from changing your circumstances. It's really that simple to change your life. We just happen to make it way too complicated. If you don't currently like your circumstances, write down where you would like your life to be 12 months from now. Then right down the first choice you need to make and three actions that you need to take to get where you want to be. Once you are done with that choice, write down the next decision you need to make and three more action steps. What you will begin to see is that you start making small steps of progress towards improving the direction of your life. Changing your circumstances does not typically come from some big, grandiose plan that shakes things up. Effective change comes from making choices, in small incremental steps, that begin to build momentum in your life. But always remember, bad choices bring bad consequences in life, business, and relationships. If you have a history of making bad choices in your life, find someone you know who has a history of making good choices, swallow your pride, and ask them to help you change your decision-making process.

I don't care how poor you are, how bad you hate your job, how empty your soul is, how bad a relationship is, how bad the neighborhood is that you live in, how bad your life has become… The ONLY reason your life stays that way is because YOU make a CHOICE to STAY there. You are better than that and should want more for your life. Start making good choices and taking the three steps necessary now and seek out the life you want. Don't let fear, comparison, or pains of the past keep you where you are. The first element in changing your circumstances is making a decision to want more for your life. Make the choice to change today.

TIME

The second Pillar that impacts your life is Time. Time is not an unlimited resource that you have the luxury of wasting. It is finite. There are only 24 hours in a day. On average, you sleep seven hours of that away, work another eight to ten, leaving seven or so hours a day to invest in making your life better. You saw in the life assessment exercise how much time you have to live the life you want.

Your clock is ticking every day, and you are either investing time wisely, or wasting it. If you are coming up short on reaching the life you want, you need to analyze how you are spending your time. I know many self-employed people who say to me, "I really need some more clients to grow my business." My question is always, "How much time did you spend this week taking action steps that will guarantee that you develop new clients?" I get a blank stare because they did nothing, but the question makes them think about how they need to invest their time each week to generate new business. Many high school and college students are wondering why their grades are what they are, and yet they spend not nearly enough time studying to be able to learn what they need to excel in their classes. If someone tells me they plan to spend about five hours a week at school for a course load of twelve hours, I would say, "Get ready to be a 'C' student." The average student cannot spend only one hour a night on school work and excel in the classroom at a level high enough to guarantee they get into college or a good job upon graduation. Great grades are definitely connected to the amount of time you spend outside the classroom on your schoolwork.

These are just two examples of how wasting your time will have a very negative impact on your ability to have a good quality of life. As with your choices, if you are not happy with your circumstances, and your life is not going in the direction that you want it to go, you need to look at how you spend your time.

I highly recommend using a good calendar app to help you manage your time. My wife and I use Calengoo. It integrates with Google calendar and allows us to share calendars in real time so we both don't overload our schedules. We put everything in our business and personal calendars, including appointments, dates, to-do's, workouts, time with our family, and vacations. Anything needing "our time", no matter how big or small is on our calendar on our phone. It makes it easy to go back and look at how we spend our time in alignment with our goals.

MONEY

The third Pillar you need to address, is how you spend your money. Money is attached to almost every part of your life because nothing is free. You pay for everything in some fashion. There are a couple of key items that you need to really, really pay attention to when it comes to money.

• Credit cards aren't trees with money hanging like fruit that you can just grab and spend with no thought of paying back. You will have to pay it back. Failure to do so will set back your life in interest payments and a credit score that takes years to build back up.

•   Your credit score is your grade that tells anyone you borrow money from what your ability is to pay them back. No matter what you are asking for a loan for, they will all access your credit score to judge your ability to pay it back. If it's low, you don't get the loan, or you pay higher interest rates. If it's good, you get the loan, and at preferable interest rates. This is the number one financial tool you need in obtaining loans of any type. Protect and monitor it religiously.

•   Be cautious of debt. Debt can be a really good thing, and it can be a really bad thing. It can also be a run-away train that forces you into bankruptcy. Secured debt, where you are buying an asset like a home, car, or something that you can sell if you ever had to in order to eliminate or minimize the debt, is not bad. The debt arrangements you need to be very cautious of are credit cards. Credit lines and other unsecured debt are potentially dangerous because you have no asset behind it to sell and pay it off. Debt can bring on financial pressures to your family, business, and relationships. Manage it wisely.

•   Have a budget with your personal life, as well as, your business life. This will help you know instantly, at any moment, if you have enough money coming in to pay for your expenses. The key to any lifestyle is to live within your financial means. If you want to increase your lifestyle, make a choice to find a way to earn more money. Don't get approved for another $5,000 limit credit card and pay $50 a month for ten years to finance your lifestyle. It's not worth it. Budgeting is easy. Get an Excel spreadsheet or piece of paper. Write down all of the income items you have coming in and total them up on a monthly basis for the next 12-months. Then write down all the expenses that you incur on a regular basis in each month and total them up. You will either have money left over or not each month. From here you can make the right decisions…do you need more income, or do you need to cut expenses for any of the next 12 months. This is a powerful process because it allows you to see if you will come up short in future months, so you can prepare to make more income, save, or cut expenses. The worst time to find out you are short $1,000 is the month you are short. Budgeting ahead resolves this stress.

Learning to manage your financial health will play a crucial role in almost every decision you make in life. Financial pressures put extreme tension and stress in any business or relationship. Learn to manage your money well. As a good friend of mine once said, "Everything's funny when you're making money." In my long life, I would have to agree 100%.

PEOPLE

I'm not going to spend very much time on the fourth Pillar because I have an entire chapter focused on the people you surround yourself with. What I will say at this point is that whomever you hang out with, you will become like. If you want to go a certain direction in life and none of the people you hang out with on a regular basis are headed that way, you will either assume their direction, or need to NOT make them a part of your everyday crowd.

ATTITUDE

Attitude is the first in my four Characteristics that you must have in order to reach your goals. When I say attitude, I mean you need to have a good attitude, that is positive, keeps you optimistic, moving forward, and works to bring people together to find solutions. This is especially true if you are a leader. As a leader, people don't go where you tell them to go. They go where you go. If you show a bad attitude, your people will have a bad attitude. If you have a "failure is not an option" attitude, your team will have a "failure is not an option" attitude. When people ask, "Who should we get to lead this project, join the team, or promote?" They aren't going to think of the person with the bad attitude. They are going to think of the person whose attitude projects hard work, a positive attitude, and is a team player. You need to check your attitude and make sure it represents someone that advances life forward. Your career and your Dash will love you for it.

ABILITY TO ADAPT

Am I about to say the word "change?" Yes, I just said that. Change is the one thing that is constant in life. If you are going to continue to grow in your life and reach new levels in your quality of life, you need to learn how to adapt and change whether you like it or not. New technologies, job requirements, and the demands on your life are changing around you every day. It is important that you learn how to adapt to those changes so the friction you feel, and experience is minimized. Remember, just because you have been a great employee for years, doesn't mean you will be a great employee in the future. You may still have the same great skill set as you had before, but the environment, technology, and demands of your position have changed, and you were unwilling to change with it. Because of your inability to adapt, you opened the door for someone new, who has the new qualities needed, to take on your position. Change is always happening in job requirements and the skills needed. If you want to maximize your success in life, work to embrace change and adapt. Be a person that says, "Yes, and we can do this!" Don't be the person who looks at every idea or innovation and says, "Yeah, BUT..."

COMMUNICATION

The third Characteristic you will need to be successful is an effective communication style. I don't want to steal my thunder for a later chapter, where I talk about your communication strategy...you just know you need a good one. You need to work at it. Lack of a good communication skill set will minimize your success in business, friendships, and relationships with your children, spouse, and friends. In life, communication is EVERYTHING...why not be great at it?

PERSEVERANCE

Throughout your life there are going to be times when it seems like a cakewalk; other times are going to feel like you have hit rock bottom and if you go any further you could be knocking on the door of hell. Remember, life is not about a destination...it's about the journey. Things will come, and things will go, including the lows in your life. You need to look at the low times in your life as an opportunity to build the strength and character that you need to do the big things in your life. Doing anything great doesn't come easy. It comes with obstacles, speed bumps, people getting in your way, and unforeseen circumstances. In order to weather the storm and come out on the other side, you need to learn that things are never as bad as we want to believe they are, and you need to focus on the things that you CAN control. This entire book is focused on giving you what you need to know in order to persevere through the pushback in your life, so you can achieve the ultimate life. If you want your Dash to be amazing, you need to be one of those people who shows others that no matter what, if you set your goals and never give up, you can achieve great success.

As you read the rest of this book, I want you to perform your Personal GDP Rating and take a picture of the *Path to the Ultimate Life* visual. Refer to them often. Keep the visual on your mobile device. I've placed a picture of it at the end of this chapter so when life begins to drift, and you feel you are not on the right path, you can pull up the visual and ask yourself, "What Pillars are out of alignment and what Characteristics do I need to work on?" These eight areas will drive every decision in your life. If one or more are out of alignment, you will feel conflict, resistance, or pain in the process of pursuing your goals. Work to keep them in alignment as you build your life plan through this book. Good luck with building the rest of your life!

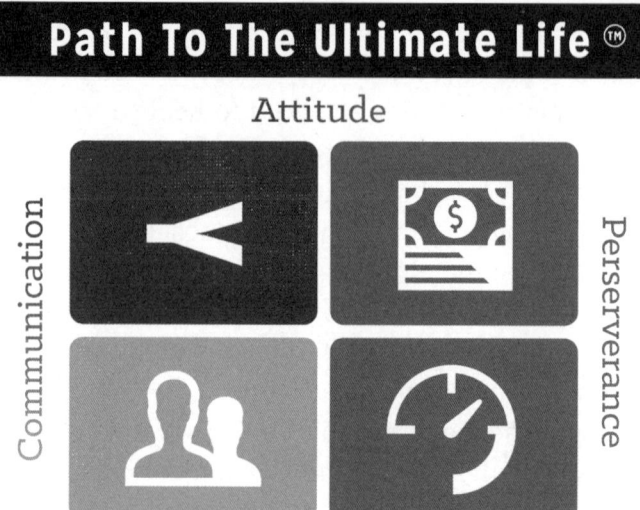

APPLICATION TO MAXIMIZE YOUR DASH

For each Pillar below, write why you feel it's a strength you have, or how you need to improve in that area:

PILLARS

CHOICES

TIME

MONEY

PEOPLE

For each Characteristic below, write why you feel it's a strength you have, or how you need to improve in that area:

CHARACTERISTICS

ATTITUDE

COMMUNICATION

ABILITY TO ADAPT

PERSEVERANCE

CHAPTER 4

HOW WILL PEOPLE IMPACT MY DASH?

"Every day people come through your life who can help you create an opportunity or solve a problem, and you choose to let them pass you by."

So, you want to know how people will be the #1 influence on how awesome your Dash is in your life? I will say from the onset, that throughout your life, having a big network of people in all walks of life will be your #1 tool to creating success in your life. People pass through your life everyday. All of them have the opportunity to have a positive impact on your circumstances. The question is, will you reach out and allow them to have that impact?

I'll make a challenge to you right now on the first page of this chapter. I want you to buy a punch counter that you hold in your hand and click every time you speak to someone on the phone, online, or in person each day for a month. This number is way more than you would ever think it is. Every day people enter your life who have their own network of people, influential contacts, expertise, talents, and resources, and who can, at some point, help you reach your goals and obtain the quality of life that you want.

Before we get deep into this book, I want you to know my life is amazing. It is amazing because of everything I have learned throughout my many ups and downs, and because of the actions I have taken from those life lessons. People look at my life now and think, "Tom, you live a great life." That may be true today through their eyes, but most don't know the path it took me to get here. You see, it hasn't always been great. I grew up in a divorced home that presented many challenges for me, and I didn't even realize it until much later in life. I didn't study well and graduated college with a 2.28 GPA. I couldn't get a job out of college because of my GPA, and I had to bartend just to make ends meet. I've been through the pains of divorce twice. I've been through the painful process and humiliation of having to file for bankruptcy. I went from being CEO of a major non-profit, to working in a sub shop, just so my family could put food on the table and pay our mortgage. I've had friends join together to pay my mortgage when I didn't have the money. I've gone to bed on Monday wondering if I was going to have enough money for groceries to feed my family come Friday. I've gone on interviews for jobs knowing I needed to be hired by the end of the month, or life was going to be very different for my family.

I've been in the deep valley of life on numerous occasions, as many of you reading this book are in, or have been in at one time. The encouraging news for you is, I came through the other end to seize the moment and achieve the quality of life that I always wanted. When I say, "quality of life", it's not a billionaire's life…it's not a millionaire's life, not even close. I'm a regular guy. I run a regular company, but I seize every moment that I can, to experience life…no matter what circumstances are in my way. My goal of this book is to help you see that it's not only the movie stars and rich and famous who can live an amazing life. Regular people live them every day. I'm living proof, and I want to show you the path to creating your own ultimate life…that leaves you feeling rewarded and fulfilled every day.

Now you may be asking yourself, "Tom, what is the ultimate life?" My friend, the ultimate life is an incredible feeling! It is a place that is, by no means perfect, because life isn't perfect, but you feel an amazing sense of joy, love, fulfillment, excitement, passion, and purpose. I've seen many living on the edge of financial struggles, and if you didn't know they were struggling financially, you would think they were rich. I've seen many with everything that money can buy, but their souls are as dry as the dessert on a hot day. You see, happiness and being rich aren't about how many zeros are in your net worth, what you own, or what your return on investment is.

Happiness and being rich are about the people you impact, the difference you make, and what gives YOU a return on life. Return on life (ROL) is a huge shift in thinking, as you look at the various ways you can spend your time and money. I have seen many who build monster bank accounts yet die lonely souls. I've seen many who invest their time and money into making a difference in others, and their life is overwhelmed with a sense of purpose and fulfillment.

Throughout this book, as you think about every aspect of your life, I want you to focus on, "What is my return on life?" and as we move forward I want you to think about a series of questions:

- Do I bring positive, or negative energy to people?
- Do people like talking to me, or wish I had never joined the conversation?
- Am I concerned with other people's lives, or am I just worried about me?
- Am I open to new, innovative thinking and ways to do things, or am I caught up in the same old way?
- When I speak, do I build people up, or do I tear them down?

In my life, I have found that generally, people treat you as you have treated them first. Your first set of comments, actions, or decisions set the stage for how people view you, treat you, and possibly help you when asked. The more people have a positive outlook about you, the more people you have at your disposal to help build and enhance your quality of life. An important step in looking at who YOUR PEOPLE are in your life, is to determine what kind of people you are attracting. YOUR PEOPLE are the people you surround yourself with on a constant basis. As you will learn in this book, YOUR PEOPLE have the most influence on who you are as a person and the direction your life takes. The answer to the questions above will help you answer the question of, "Who are YOUR PEOPLE?" If you don't like the people you are attracting, and you feel they are holding back in living the ULTIMATE LIFE, you might need to look in the mirror and make some changes in YOU. As you change, you will see YOUR PEOPLE change. Some will leave your life because they are unwilling to grow and change, and others will mature into a group who totally engage your life in a positive way. We will talk in depth about this later in the book.

After you have looked at yourself, you then need to figure out "who are my people." I have found in my life that no matter what level of life you are operating in, how old you are, what your circumstances are, or if you work for yourself or a business, if you are going to maximize your quality of life both personally and professionally, it is imperative that you have the right people who are running in the same direction as your life goals and dreams.

Think about it. With the rate of change in today's environment, it is crucial that you are surrounded by a network of people who you can instantly reach out to, and who can help you achieve your goals when needed. If you work for a company, you need to have three to four companies that you can call, who have said to you, "If you ever decide to leave your company, give me a call." If you are ever fired for any reason, you have a place to land and protect your financial position and family security.

If you are an owner of a company, you need to have a dozen or so people who are great at what they do, and that you know would come work for you if one of your key people left for any reason. This will help protect your service to your customers and maintain the financial security of your company.

If you are a college student, you need to network with business owners and executives, so that the moment you graduate, you have an immediate job to walk in to. Wouldn't that be awesome!

If you are a busy single mom or dad, it is an amazing

feeling to have a list of trusted people in your phone who can pick your kids up, babysit, and help you at a moment's notice. I've been a single father with young children, and really feel the emotions and challenges that single parents go through...it isn't easy and is a full-time job all in itself.

No matter what your mode of life, whether personal or professional, the more people you have around you who want you to achieve your life goals, the easier and more successful your life is going to be. It's like money...almost. Money isn't everything, but it sure makes your life easier. People are in that same boat, except I would contend that people ARE EVERYTHING, because they can have such an amazing impact on your life if you let them in. That is what this whole book is about. Along your journey through this book, we are going to look inside and touch almost every area of your life to help you make the necessary changes to reach the quality of life that you want.

If you are a college student, GET READY. If you are unemployed, GET READY. If you are a single mom or dad, GET READY. If you are unhappy with your current circumstances, GET READY. If you are already successful and want more out of life, GET READY. In each chapter of this journey, you will be filled with wisdom and insight, and read stories that I have assimilated throughout my life. I've had the fortunate pleasure of having some of the most amazing mentors, business owners, and speakers impart on me powerful truths that have paved the way to my incredible life experiences, happiness, and memories. At the end of each chapter, you will find exercises called, "Application to the Dash," and "Action Steps to the Dash." These are to help you think through each chapter and put down on paper practical action steps that you can implement to make the necessary changes in your life.

If you want more out of life, GET READY. Get ready for an amazing journey. Get ready to roll up your sleeves. Get ready to dig into your life. Get ready to make positive changes in your life, that will carry you to the "promised land" called the ULTIMATE LIFE that is filled with joy, love, self-worth, fulfillment, passion, purpose, and most importantly...MAKE YOUR OBITUARY NOT SUCK.

CHAPTER 5

WHO ARE "YOUR PEOPLE?"

"Just because someone is family, doesn't give them the right to treat you with disrespect. Friends who treat you with respect and human decency, are better to have in your life than family who abuse the privilege of being family."

In your life, you have two circles of people around you. One group has an enormous impact on your Dash. The other has little to minimal impact on your Dash. You have your inner circle (YOUR PEOPLE), which are those who you count on, run with, and allow input into your life. You also have your outer circle (NOT YOUR PEOPLE), those who offer little-to-no positive impact on your life, and in many cases, are directly trying to sabotage your success in life.

Being in the inner circle or outer circle is not determined by family status, if you are a friend, or how close you may be with someone. Which circle people are in is determined by their comments, actions, and decisions made that have any impact on your quality of life. You want to conduct yourself in a way that maximizes the number of "YOUR PEOPLE" in the inner circle who are making comments, decisions, and actions that are having a positive impact on the quality of your personal and professional life.

When I say surrounded by "YOUR PEOPLE," this means being surrounded with the right people who have a passion for your well-being…your best interest and have a desire to see you do well in life. They purposefully don't make comments, actions, or decisions that have a lasting negative impact on the well-being of your life. This isn't to say they don't ever make a hard decision, offer tough love comments, or actions that you are not happy with. If they are YOUR PEOPLE in your inner circle, generally tough issues are ones you have openly discussed and have determined that everyone is going to have to take a little on the chin. Sometimes making the right decision isn't always a happy decision, but you make the decision knowing each party has differing opinions, and you each respect that decision. YOUR PEOPLE make decisions with a level of care, trust, and respect for you.

The next question you may be asking is, "Tom, who are my people?" That is another great question. You need to re-alize that you will never make it through life living on an is-land by yourself. People are always going to have an impact on your quality of life at some level. The question is, "When people make comments, decisions, or actions that could have any impact on the quality of your life, do they make a decision, comment, or action that has a positive impact or negative impact on you?" People tend to put emphasis on decisions made by those closest to them, like family and friends. Every day, people on your fringe, make decisions without you around, and those decisions have a good or bad impact on you. People on your fringe could be employees, co-workers, customers, or industry colleagues. The way they think about you, how you conduct yourself, and how you treat them, will play a major role in their decisions, comments, or actions that impact you.

YOUR PEOPLE should include family members, customers, friends, employees, or anyone who can make a comment, decision, or action that could influence the direction of your quality of life. Practically every minute of every day, people influence and impact the direction of your life at varying levels. Don't get me wrong, you cannot and will not make everyone you encounter happy, and not everyone will be YOUR PEOPLE. They have their own personal issues that they are dealing with that will prevent them from lining up with you. However, the way you conduct yourself, your energy, your attitude, the things you say, and how you treat people, will work to maximize the number of people who want to be YOUR PEOPLE. Your goal should be to conduct yourself in a way that helps to increase your inner circle of YOUR PEOPLE so that you maximize the experiences, memories, and quality of life in your personal and professional life.

On a day-to-day basis, there are generally five groups of people who make up your interactions. These people have consistent contact and influence on your life at some level. I have broken them down below in a graphic with a short explanation of each one afterward.

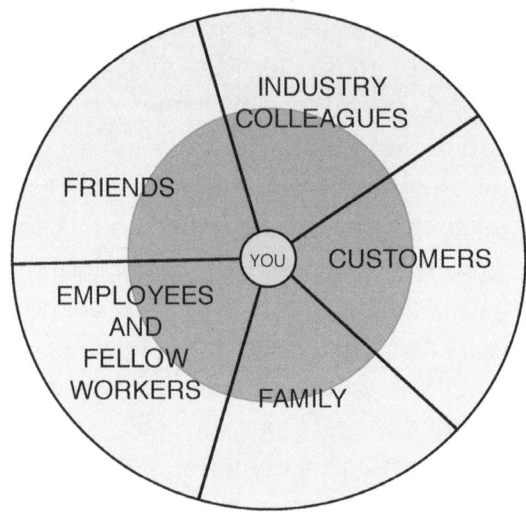

Inner Circle: YOUR People
Outer Circle: Everyone Else

FAMILY

Family has a direct impact on your life because they are in it every day. There is an emotional bond that makes their connection with you very personal, and decisions deep-rooted. You would think that family would be the easiest people to help you maximize your quality of your Dash because of that personal bond. Sadly, more often than not, family can take advantage of you the fastest, or encourage you to make bad decisions because of that personal bond. Some family members know they can use their personal connection to influence you to make a bad decision because you would never think they would want to take advantage of you. I've witnessed family members borrowing money from other family members, knowing they have no intention of repaying the money. They took advantage of their family relationship and leveraged it to get the money they felt they needed for whatever purpose. Bad decision to lend the money. I've seen older parents make bad choices due to influence of their older children, because the child leveraged their relationship under the notion, "If you make that choice, I'll never speak to you again." Never make a choice based upon this statement. Just because someone is your spouse, child, or close family member, doesn't give them the right to treat you unfairly, disrespectfully, or force you to make a bad choice. YOUR PEOPLE should never make that a condition as a part of a major decision that has potentially negative consequences on your quality of life.

On the flipside, family members also make certain decisions based upon their relationship with you. You get the benefit of the doubt. There is a trust and care that supersedes any thought of directing you to make a bad choice that could have negative consequences in your life. You need to understand and be able to discern both, so you know when to say "no" to the family member, no matter how hard it is to say no. You should say "yes" only to those family members who have your best interest at heart, not their own agenda in mind.

FRIENDS

Friends are great. They come, they go, and like a soap opera, when you pick back up it's like you never left. However, like family members, they can, and will use the personal bond for their benefit. They can be "time suckers" if you allow them to pull you into their daily drama. Stay close to the ones whose actions, decisions, and comments align with where you want to go in life. This doesn't mean to ignore the time wasters. You need to spend time with them, listen to them, and try and help them make good choices, but don't allow them to dominate your time in their negative world. Remember the four Pillars. Time is an asset you cannot recoup. Once it's gone, it's gone. Don't waste it.

EMPLOYEES AND FELLOW WORKERS

Whether you are the business owner, or an employee of a company, employees and fellow workers are like your daytime family. You probably spend more time with your co-workers on an annual basis than you do your family, given you spend eight to ten hours a day with them five days a week. It is crucial you get to know them and let them know you at some level, so they will be YOUR PEOPLE. Problems at work will play themselves out at home if you aren't careful. A bad day at the office can cause a bad night at home for your spouse/partner and/or children depending on your attitude when you walk in the door. If your employees are YOUR PEOPLE, then they are working to create a positive and encouraging work environment that you enjoy. Remember, home life is tough for many, and if you help create a very energetic and positive environment at work, your co-workers or employees will all want to be YOUR PEOPLE.

CUSTOMERS

Whether you are an owner, sales person, or general staff, customers are a huge influence in our life. Each day, they make decisions to buy your products and services, as well as, refer your company to others. As referrals and purchases go up, companies thrive, and so do their employees. As referrals and purchases decline, companies do poorly, and jobs are eliminated. In my opinion, every single employee plays a role in the customer experience. It is imperative that you have a good attitude and bring your best to work every day to serve your customer, and to make sure they are one of YOUR PEOPLE. My motto is: "Every person in a company should treat customers as if they are the only reason they do business with your company."

INDUSTRY/COLLEGE PEERS

Industry and college peers are huge in our process of networking, business, and professional development. Industry and college peers can refer business, partner with you on large projects, provide valuable information, resources, or connect you to someone else who can help you capitalize on an opportunity. This group of people will definitely make choices based on how they interact with you, based upon your integrity, how you treat them, and how you help them. When it comes to creating an awesome quality of life, this group of people plays a huge role. You will want to have a perpetual plan of increasing this group of people as YOUR PEOPLE each year. Remember, many of your friends in your industry, as well as college, will rise to be Presidents and key executives of companies, or very influential people who can help further your professional or personal life. (I will speak later in the book on how to be a master networker.)

Bottom line, every day you have five different groups of people who are impacting your quality of life in a positive or negative way. YOUR PEOPLE have a positive impact on you. Everyone else has a negative, or no impact on your life. Your goal should be to live your life in such a manner so as to maximize the number of YOUR PEOPLE who will maximize your life experiences, create memories, grow your financial security, and increase the quality of your life.

APPLICATION TO MAXIMIZE YOUR DASH

Which group of people do you need to work on expanding in your "YOUR PEOPLE" circle?
- o   Family
- o   Friends
- o   Employees/Co-Workers
- o   Customers
- o   Industry/College Peers

What do you feel are your biggest challenges to expanding "Your People"?

ACTION STEPS TO THE ULTIMATE LIFE

Write down the two outside influences you will need to confront to expand "Your People." How will you deal with them?

What is your action item to implement in the next 30 days to make positive change and begin expanding "Your people"?

CHAPTER 6

ARE YOU A BULLY OR BUILDER OF PEOPLE?

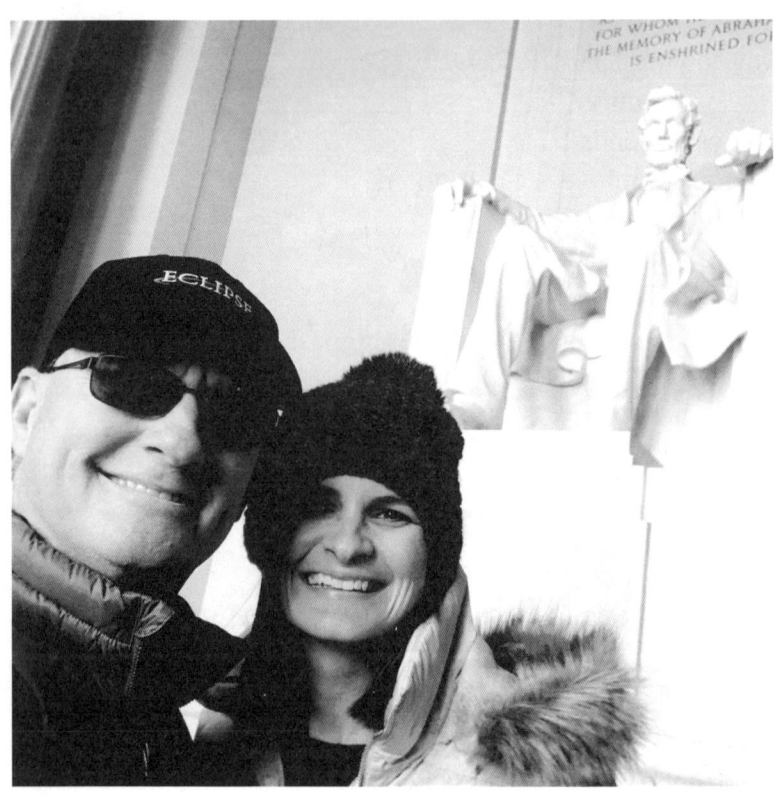

"What do people lack in their life that makes them feel like they have to bully people to get what they want in life? Bullies divide people. Builders bring people together."

As people enter or pass in your Dash, you will always be characterized as one of two types of people: A builder of people, or a bully of people. You can be seen as someone who is neither, but generally with all interactions, you are either a builder or bully.

Builders are people who have a desire to see people do well. They extend a little grace because they know life isn't perfect and neither are people or processes. Bullies on the other hand can't wait for you to screw up. You know who I'm talking about. They are the person in the meeting who always sees the glass as half empty and impresses on you how empty it is, even when you show them data that their thinking is incorrect. They are the person who emotionally beats you up in a rude fashion in negotiations. Their goal is not to have a win-win scenario, but a win-lose scenario, because they feel good when someone else feels bad. They are the person who makes cutting remarks about you, because in order for them to feel worthy in life, they must use harsh words to make someone else feel bad.

Some people have a natural part of their DNA to be either a builder or bully of people. It's in their personality and what they grew up around. However, you need to look in the mirror and ask yourself, do you need to improve in this area.

So, I want to ask you, "When you look at how you treat people, do you build them up or bully them around?" It doesn't matter if you are selling to customers, managing employees, babysitting kids, or trying to get your boss, parents, or spouse to see things a certain way. How you treat people is at least 50% responsible for getting them to engage, be inspired, or motivated to do what you want.

If you aren't getting the things you need from people around you, you need to ask yourself the question, "How do I treat people? Am I a BULLY or a BUILDER of people?" It's not the sole reason you may not be getting your way, but it plays a huge role in how people respond. A couple of other questions to ponder on this issue are:

- Do you feel you need to emotionally push people

around to get what you want?

- Are you more concerned with being right, than having the right decision made?
- Are you comfortable facilitating the right decision versus being the right decision?
- What is it in your past that makes you feel like you have to bully people to get what you want?

One thing we need to understand is, life is way too hard around us on a day-to-day basis to have a boss, volunteer, fellow employee, family member, or anyone we work with creating unnecessary conflict in our life because of something they lack. That's right. I've found in my life that most emotional bullies are that way because of something they lack internally or emotionally.

I want you to try this exercise with a friend: The next time you are with someone, have them throw an idea out to you. Then both take turns brainstorming how to make the idea better by starting every sentence with, "Yes but…" Once you have worked through your ideas, do it again, but start each idea with, "Yes and…" You will find that as you start with "Yes but…" your mind can't help but think of negative things to say. On the other hand, when you do the exercise a second time through and start with "Yes and…" you feel like you are free to explore every idea that comes to mind. You see, by simply changing one single word, you were able to change your attitude within the conversation, allowing you to empower people, not tear them down.

Every person you meet, you have the opportunity to provide hope and encouragement, and create transformation in their lives. Yet, in this "feel good" state of transforming people's lives, some feel the need to bully or run over people to get it done.

- Is it because you have insecurities?

- Do you feel inferior to those you lead or work with?
- Do you feel you have to "look good" in front of your peers?
- Are there issues in your past, with parents or other relationships that are unresolved?

Hear me out on this one phrase: *"When PERSONALITIES get in the way of the PURPOSE, that is the beginning of the end of the PURPOSE."* You see, bullies are more about "being right," rather than doing "what's right." Builders of people are about seeking "what's right," rather than "being right."

Knowing this, why do people continue to bully those around them to get what they want, when it does nothing but serve the purpose of tearing apart a potentially amazing idea or team? A couple of questions I always ask people about themselves are:

- If a small group of people see you coming down the hallway, do they look to scatter before you get to them for fear of your wrath? ...Or do they hang out because they want to have a moment of your time because you provide a positive energy in their life?
- When people leave your presence, do they feel better or worse about themselves?
- Do people feel lifted up or stressed out the moment you enter a room they're in?

Don't get me wrong, there is a time to be firm, but to be a bully at every turn does yourself, those you lead, work with, or hang out with, a big disservice. Being a bully divides people. Being a builder of people brings people together.

When trying to think of an acronym that could easily be remembered on how to treat people you connect with in any scenario, especially those you lead, I discovered this: "I **C.A.T.E.R.** to people so they will maximize my experience in my Dash." **C.A.T.E.R.** stands for the following:

Confidence - Impress *confidence* on people around you by having *confidence* in them.

Authority - Give people the *authority* they need to get the job done.

Trust - Let your actions demonstrate that you *trust* that they can make the right choices.

Empower - Don't micromanage people. You tell them the "What" and let them figure out the "How."

Respect - Show r*espect* and allow people the latitude to fail or succeed.

I'm confident if you live by the philosophy of **C.A.T.E.R.**ing to anyone in your life, you will see an exciting team of people that will develop around you, that will help you accomplish whatever goals you establish in your Dash.

Keep this in mind, people want to be a part of someone's life who they feel empowers them. BULLIES get in the way of empowerment and create no positive progress for anyone. BUILDERS of people drive empowerment and make people's lives feel worthwhile, to the point that they will want to do anything for you.

Throughout this book, you will learn the keys to living your ultimate life, how to treat people fairly, and how to network with them to be a builder of people.

Remember, PEOPLE are the number one key to you maximizing your experiences in your Dash. Act and choose wisely.

APPLICATION TO MAXIMIZE YOUR DASH

If you are honest with yourself, do you build people up, or are you a bully? If so, why?

What makes you want to bully another person?

Do you feel it's okay for someone else to be right and you wrong?

How do you feel in a disagreement of any type, when someone tells you new information that you weren't aware of, which proves you wrong? Do you admit to being wrong and engage in positive dialogue? …Or do you continue defending your position and create undue stress in the conversation?

Are you negative to people just to be negative and to get under their skin? If yes, why?

ACTION STEPS TO MAXIMIZE YOUR DASH

At your next meeting with friends or co-workers, try the "Yes but" and the "Yes and" exercise.

Write down three ways that you can change your attitude, words you say, or actions toward people, that will make you a better builder of people.

CHAPTER 7

THE STAGES OF YOUR PROFESSIONAL LIFE

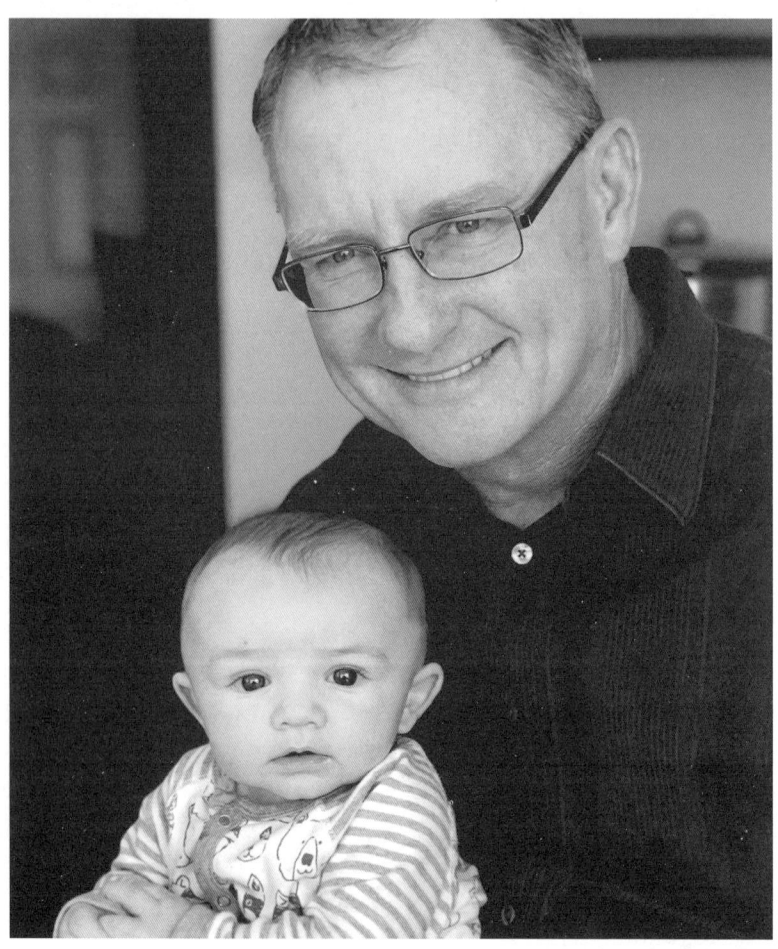

"Two things that will hold you back in life will be comparing yourself to others, and the inability to be content in your current stage of life. Love who you are, be content with where you are, while striving to improve your quality of life."

One of my biggest desires in writing this book is to share my journey towards achieving a great quality of life, and what I feel are the keys to success in everyday living. I've talked to many people who have read books or attended keynote speeches by famous billionaires on the keys to success. Most people listen in, but they tune out how to apply those keys to their life because they feel that those people live in a "dream world", and they can't relate to their life. Only a small percentage of people ever achieve the "dream world" level of life, where financial pressures are not a day-to-day concern to them. I wanted to write this book as a "regular person", working in the "real world", to inspire other everyday people to have that same energetic, rewarding, and fun-filled quality of life that we feel only billionaires enjoy.

I once gave my son a card for his birthday that read, "Life isn't about money. But it sure makes life easier." The more successful you are in your professional career or business, the more freedom and opportunities you will have to maximize your quality of life personally. You don't have to be a millionaire or billionaire to experience the best in life, but you do need to have "enough" to make it happen. You decide what is enough.

When you look at your professional career or business life, there are nine stages that everyone fits into at any given point in time. I will outline these nine stages in just a bit, but if you are like most, you are in pursuit of moving up to the next stage throughout your life to increase your financial opportunities or resources.

No matter what age you are, there are three elements you must have in order to maximize your opportunity, growth, and income potential in any of the stages of life I describe later in this chapter. They are:

- Some level of education past high school. This can

be a certificate program, technical schools, or a college education.
- You need to have a skill that is valued by the market-place; that is in demand and is needed.
- You need to perform your skill with excellence.

If you lack one of these three, you will always limit your opportunities to maximize your income potential in life. I would take some time to think about these three elements and analyze how you stand with all three. Everyone, and I mean everyone, has gifts and talents to accomplish great achievements in life. Seek yours out, further your education to have the knowledge you need, and pursue your skill with excellence so the marketplace wants to pay you top dollar for your skillset and services.

As you ponder those thoughts, do you remember the best advice you ever received from someone? Advice that spoke into your soul, that allowed you to breathe and say, "Life is going to be okay." I can remember mine like it was yesterday. I was the ripe old age of 19…full of life and energy, in the middle of taking a semester off from college to relax after 13 years of being in school and was one of the top bartenders at a major entertainment complex in Orlando, Florida. I loved bartending because it taught me everything I needed to know about communication skills and meeting people's needs. Each day, I had the opportunity to mix, mingle, and converse with everyone from homeless people looking for a glass of water, to high-flying Wall Street financial planners enjoying happy hour, to millionaires waiting to meet with the owner. As I struck up conversations with each person I met, I would seek to tap into their knowledge…especially those who looked like they had achieved some level of success and were living a good quality of life. Those that I perceived had the type of success that I was looking for in my life, I would ask for their best advice for a 19-year-old in college.

The number one piece of advice came from a man who owned his own company. I chatted with him a fair amount throughout the night, laughing and enjoying some great conversation. At the end of the night, he knew I was serious about wanting to be more than a bartender, and he asked me to come to the end of the bar for a few moments. When I got to the end of the bar, he put his arm around me and gave me some of the best advice that I still live by…even today. He proceeded to share with me that life happens every day whether you show up or not. He stated, *"Life is a long ride. As a 19-year-old, don't be in such a hurry to get to your destination without enjoying the ride. Pick your pace of life that is comfortable with the lifestyle that you want to lead. Don't be in a hurry to get to success. If you work hard, surround yourself with good people, and don't burn bridges, success will come. Set goals that are specific enough to keep you focused, but general enough to be flexible to seize the opportunities that come out of nowhere. Don't ever assume that you cannot do a job. We are always more talented than we want to believe."* I thanked him for his advice, shook his hand, and said good night. This man never really knew the impact that that short five minutes meant in my life. I let what he said sink in, and the whole next week I began to think about my future related to the statements he made:

- Setting goals that are specific enough to keep you focused, but general enough to seize opportunities that may come our way.
- Don't be in a hurry to arrive at the destination of success. Enjoy the journey along the way to success.

After looking at my life, and where I wanted to be in the future, I set the following specific goals:

GOAL 1

I wanted to graduate college by the time I was 25. I was in no hurry to graduate. I was going to work for the next 50 years of my life with not nearly as much freedom to enjoy life as I did as a college student. Why graduate at 22 and jump into a career that would demand so much of my life so soon? I wanted to work on being me, and enriching my life, instead of serving a boss. I figured the better and more mature I was coming out of college, the better and more mature I would be as a professional in the workplace.

GOAL 2

I wanted to get my first career job out of college by 25 and work there for five years. As I studied employment ads for management at 19, I noticed that all of them wanted five years of management experience. If five years was the magic number, then I wanted to land at a company after college, and stay there five years to get the best, real world experience to match up with the knowledge I had learned in college. Along with getting my first job, I had a desire to find a wife and start a family. I liked the idea of having children in my twenties, because once they were off to college, my wife and I would be in our mid-forties, and still young enough to enjoy life with our kids as young adults.

GOAL 3

Noticing that there was a pretty big pay jump for those who had a college degree, and at least five years of management experience with the same company, I wanted to land a job opportunity that could accelerate my financial opportunity significantly by the time I was 30.

GOAL 4

I wanted to work for 10 years in my career, and do it with such excellence, that when I turned 40 I would be able to step up to another level and boost my financial opportunity and professionalism again. I viewed this job as my last job in life…one that could carry me into my retirement years… lasting a good 20 to 25 years. During this ten-year period, I wanted to be successful enough at what I did professionally, that one day I could speak professionally, and others would pay to hear my success story. As my professional career was blossoming, I had a huge desire to be the best father and husband to my family as well.

GOAL 5

I wanted to begin speaking at some point in my forties and write an inspiring book about success in life and business.

Once I had these five goals down on paper, I now had what I felt were achievable goals that allowed me to have a great balance to enjoy the journey of life, reach a destination I deemed successful, and were focused, yet flexible.

I'm sure that with goals written out like that, you are probably asking yourself, "So how did those work out for you?" Great question! I am now in my fifties…over 30 years after setting those goals, and here is what my resume looks

like:
- I graduated Florida State University at 26
- I got my first career job at 25
- I worked at first career job for six years
- I got married at 24
- I had my children at 25 and 27
- I leapt in to my second professional position at 31, which doubled my financial opportunities
- I rose to the top of my industry, landing my current position as CEO of an international trade association at age 41
- I began to speak at industry conferences at 47
- I wrote my previous book, *How to Get People to Scream Your Name and Beg for More* at 50

When you look at my goals and the path my life has taken, it is amazing how closely my path followed my written goals. Don't get the notion that it was all easy and rosy. There were numerous hiccups along the way, like divorce, bankruptcy, taking too much risk, and learning a few lessons the hard way. How you deal with that difficulty will decide how quickly you get back on track with your goals and your plan. These bumps in the road are never life-ending experiences. They are learning opportunities that help you know what not to do in the future. Not everything happened in the exact year and in the exact way I had planned, but they were pretty close because I stayed true to the flexible timeline I had put into place. The most amazing thing about my life is that my career in association management, which I have enjoyed for over 20 years now, is one that I never even knew existed when I graduated from college. This speaks to the part about being flexible with your goals and plans. Leave them open for unexpected business opportunities and career paths that you didn't even know existed.

The moral of the story is: If you want to build a good quality of life in your future, you must set goals that fit the type of lifestyle that you want to lead, have an executable plan to make it happen at each stage of life, and pay attention to the **Path to the Ultimate Life** visual as your guide. We will talk more about this throughout the book.

Now back to the nine stages that I mentioned earlier in this chapter. When we talk about stages of professional life, everyone is in one. Just as there are five groups of people who will have direct impact on your life day-to-day, there are nine stages of professional life. Everyone is in one of these stages at any given point in time. Following are the descriptions of the stages of life and a visual graphic:

College or Unemployed
These are people who are either furthering their education to start a career or are not currently working.

Job Transition
These are people who are working for temp agencies, or in a job that will end due to a life change. Many college students who work in retail or food services fit this stage, and then move on to the next level once they graduate.

Entry Level Career
This is typically the first level of professional work for college students, as well as professionals starting in a new career or with a new company. The goal of an entry level position is to get your foot in the door, so you can prove your work ethic and value to the company, thereby allowing you to move up quickly within the organization.

Middle Management

This stage of life is the one that happens after you typically pass that five-year mark of experience in the company, or in leading people.

Upper Management
This stage is when you are promoted to a CXO position, like CFO, CIO, or CMO, are in charge of many people, and have a high level of responsibility.

CEO or President of Company You Do Not Own
This stage is typically after many years of working up the corporate ladder and you are responsible for the overall executive decisions and financial success of the company.

Self-Employed
This stage fits the one-person companies like consultants, real estate agents, and personal fitness trainers. These are people who had an idea or a talent and decided they did not want to work for anyone else, so they struck out on their own.

Company Owner
This stage generally happens to many self-employed people whose company grows, and they have to hire more people, or executives of other companies who decide to open a company on their own.

Super Star Dream Status
These are movie stars, professional athletes, and other public figures who have achieved amazing success and wealth.

Retired

This stage typically happens later in life and is when we decide that we have enough financial resources to walk away from one of the stages we are working in above. This stage only happens to those who plan early enough in life for it to actually happen. If you don't plan for how you will have enough money in the bank "working for you" when you quit working, then your only financial resource will be Social Security, at about $1,000 to $2,000 a month. You will not like this lifestyle option...I promise. We will talk about this later in the book.

So, which stage are you in? Do you have a desire to move to the next stage? Do you have a plan to keep you moving to the next stage? If not, you should.

Until you know where you want to go, analyze where you are, and put a plan in place to make up the difference, or you will continue to spin your wheels in the same place, and wonder years later why you have made no progress.

STAGES OF LIFE
College or Unemployed
Job Transition
Entry Level Career
Middle Management
Upper Management
CEO/President of Company You Don't Own
Self Employed
CEO or President of Company You Own
Super Star Status
Retirement

Now that you have a handle on the importance of establishing some goals for yourself, and what stage of life you are in professionally, I want to conclude this chapter talking about the two things that will keep you from achieving your goals and having a rewarding quality of life. Those two things are "comparison" and "caring what other people think about you."

I know there are people reading this book who are constantly comparing their life to others who are in a higher, more successful stage of life, and trying to play catch-up. There are people reading this book who allow "what others think of them" to dictate way too much of their decision-making processes. They are working too hard to buy things they don't need, to create a lifestyle to impress people who don't care about them. They aren't a part of "YOUR PEOPLE" as discussed in the earlier chapter. If you live your life constantly comparing yourself to what other people have, and let that drive your decision-making process, that will create unnecessary stress and financial pressures in your life. You will continue to work more hours, to make more money, to keep up. Financial stress is one of the worst stresses that you can have in your life. Don't create it for yourself or your family.

I want to encourage you to be content, but not satisfied, in the stage of life where you are, and understand that you are on a journey. I firmly believe that everyone is exactly where they are supposed to be, at each stage of their life, in any given moment. Love where you are, be the best in that moment, and have a desire to be moving toward the next stage of life. If you are always distracted with your destination, you will never be the best at each stage of life. One of my life principles is to NOT be the best "once" I get to the destination, but TO BE THE BEST at every stage of life along the journey.

When I got my first job as a landscaper at an apartment complex in 1978, I wanted to make sure that I was the best at taking care of the complex. I loved hearing tenants say that they loved how the apartment complex looked...so clean and well landscaped. When I was a bartender in college, I strived to be the best bartender in the entertainment complex of 50-plus bartenders. At one point, myself and another bartender that I worked with became known as the "A-Team."

As I have pursued my professional career, I have worked to be the best at my profession every single day. In 2012, I was honored by my association executive peers as the Association Executive of the Year. You see my point? You can't wait until you reach your dream job to be the best at what you do. It is imperative that you work to be the best at every stage of your professional life. Your greatness will maximize your experiences and fulfillment in your Dash at every stage of life.

Be inspired and challenged to keep progressing forward to the next stage of life that can improve your financial resources and have a positive impact on your family and your ability to help others. You have greatness inside of you... everyone does. You just need to discover it and let it out.

Every year I see people working hard to plan for a future they cannot predict. I say, "Quit trying to plan for a future you cannot predict and create the future you want."

Don't let what other people think about you drive your decision-making processes. If you do, you will live your life with insecurity, unhappiness, and in some cases, depression, because you'll feel like you can never make everyone happy. FREE yourself from that! Know that you will NEVER make everyone happy. Some people, because of who they are, will never like you, or think positively about the decisions you make. This is more about who they are, than who you are. Don't give them that control of your life.

What I know is that God doesn't make junk. You were created for success and you have the freedom to make success happen in your life...if, and only if, you have a deep enough desire for it, want to work hard for it, make good choices to get there, and treat people right along the way.

For the rest of this book, I am going to share with you 14 life-changing key words that begin with the letter "P." I have found in my life, that when these 14 areas of life are all in alignment, you experience amazing levels of joy and fulfillment in all areas of your life. When any of them are out of alignment, that is where conflict, unhappiness, selfishness, and bad decisions creep into daily life.

Once you have worked through the 14 "P's", I will share with you the 11 keys that you need to focus on to maximize your experiences between the numbers in your Dash. The question is, "Do you want it?" Do you want to wake up with a smile every day...or with anger? Do you want people to help you when you call...or let it go to voicemail because they prefer not to talk to you? Do you want people to see you as someone who is a positive influence in their life... or someone who sucks the life out of them with negativity when you are around?

The great thing about today, is that it can be the start of the rest of your life! If you live life frustrated and blaming others for your lot in life...STOP. It's your life...not others.

Read the rest of this book and put actions to the areas we will discuss, and finish life well. Have a desire to wake up with a smile, be a positive influence on everyone you touch, and enrich the lives of others. As I heard in a movie once, "Stop praying for a miracle and BE THE MIRACLE." Before that though...you need to work on you. Good luck in the journey.

APPLICATION TO MAXIMIZE YOUR DASH

What stage of life are you in?

o   College or Unemployed
o   Job Transition
o   Entry Level Career
o   Middle Management
o   Upper Management
o   CEO or President of Company You Dont Own
o   Self Employed
o   CEO or President of Company You Own
o   Super Star Status
o   Retired

What are your biggest outside influences that you will need to confront in order to improve your current stage, or move to the next stage of life?

What are your biggest challenges to moving to the next stage? If your current stage is awesome, what are your challenges to making it an even better quality of life?

ACTION STEP TO MAXIMIZE YOUR DASH

What is your action item to implement in the next 30 days to make positive change and improve your current life stage or move to the next stage?

CHAPTER 8

DEFINING YOUR PURPOSE

"Having no purpose in life is like trying to drive from Miami to Seattle with no map.

You live in a constant state of, where are we?"

Webster's dictionary defines PURPOSE as "the reason for which something is done or created, or for which something exists." The key words here for you are, "for which something exists." No matter what stage of life you are in, my question for you is, why do you exist each day? The most successful and happiest people have figured this out. When I say, "successful people", that doesn't equate to dollar signs in the bank. It equates to people who are experiencing a great quality of life that is meaningful in their heart, mind, and soul…they are experiencing joy, love, and happiness. A quality of life where everyone around them feels the positive energy and encouragement they bring with them every day. These people have a center focus on why they were created, why they exist, and whom they were created to serve. The heat of a bad day at the office, or a supervisor screaming at them doesn't get them down because their "purpose in life" is much bigger than that one moment, so that moment will most likely not mean anything one week later.

I've witnessed people who have everything you could ever imagine financially, yet their soul feels empty, and no one wants to be around them. I've heard stories of rich people who had less than 50 people at their funeral, and a janitor who had over 500 people attend their funeral. Which of these two people reached the most people for good in their life?

Being rich and successful is not about a number, it's about the legacy you leave between the day you were born and the day you pass on…Your Dash. Oh yes, you are going to pass on. The question is when, and how do you want your life to be remembered? That is the point of this book.

Everyone needs a purpose in life. Purpose provides you with focus. It provides stability. It provides an answer to the question that everyone asks at some point in their life, "Why am I here?" In my opinion, everyone has been born with a certain set of talents and passion to help serve a specific set of people or cause in their life. If you don't think PURPOSE is a big deal, then why do so many people reach 40, 50, even 60 years of age and look back at their life asking themselves after all that time, "What has my life meant? Why was I put here? Would it even matter if I disappeared?" It's crazy to have seemingly wasted all those years before you began to seek out your true purpose in life. It's why I strongly encourage all young people reading this book to define your purpose while you are young. Purpose brings strength to your career, business decisions, as well as, every personal relationship.

Don't get me wrong, if you are over 40, you haven't wasted all those years, but it can sure feel like it if you wait until after 49 to start thinking about, "Why am I here?" No matter what your age, the time is NOW to figure it out.

If you lead people at any level, when those you lead know you have a purpose, it gives them a confidence in you because they know there is stability there. They know you have direction…that you aren't just making decisions on a whim. They know you have an inner strength circled around a central purpose for your life.

I can remember when I discovered my purpose. It was January 1995. I was on my knees beside my bed in some sense of panic, emotional pain, and anxiety. I was trying to make sense of and figure out where my life had disappeared to. I was 31 years old, and a year ago that month I had a great family, wife, children, church and job. I was living what I thought was "the dream", but as the year progressed, it all began to come apart. My wife asked for a divorce and my employer let me go. Overnight, within a year, my wife was gone, I was separated from my kids, I had no job, and I had financial obligations of child support and credit card debt that I thought I could never pay off.

As I was on the floor beside my bed in deep emotional pain, I was trying to make sense of everything. I kept second-guessing myself. I questioned everything about myself and wanted to know how everything that was so good, could go so bad inside of a year. What was my existence? Why was this happening? The pain I was experiencing was immense. When looking at my situation, I knew one thing for sure, I didn't want anyone I came in contact with in my life to experience that same pain. My life purpose was born that week.

My purpose became: to encourage and engage people in a conversation about their life, to help them reach their maximum potential, to motivate them to live a deeper and more rewarding life free of emotional pain.

I wanted to dig into people's lives at all levels to get to know their story. As I hear pain in their life, I wanted to see how I could help to encourage them through my experiences, or to turn them to someone who could help them. What I learned is that, most times people just need someone to listen to them. I have lived this out in full force since I was 31 and love every chance I get to sit and listen to someone's story to this day.

I want to encourage you to look into your soul and find your purpose in life. If your life doesn't have any worries in it, or you are young and have never thought about your purpose in life, don't wait until the rug is pulled out from underneath you in life to start asking the serious questions, "why are you here?" Start asking them today so your life can be more fulfilling.

If you are in a set of crazy circumstances like a failing marriage, financial issues, challenges with children, or work-related issues, then start thinking about your purpose today. Once you find your purpose, all of your challenges will begin to have clarity and a path of solutions will become visible. I'm here to tell you that you can be better than where you currently are…you can rise above your circumstances to be so much more, and you can begin to truly experience fulfillment in life and work. You can achieve the ultimate quality of life on a day-to-day basis, if you take the first step and define your purpose in life.

So, my challenge to you is to define your purpose this week. Here are a few questions to contemplate as you look into your soul for purpose:

- What brings the most meaning to your life?
- What people do you love to serve?
- What cause do you feel deeply connected to, and want to help?
- What life experiences have you had that have prepared you to serve?
- What gets you excited when you see the progress?
- Where do you feel the most reward when it's accomplished?
- What gifts and talents do you possess that could help others?

Remember… purpose isn't about serving yourself…it's about serving others. As Zig Ziglar said, "If you help enough people get what they want in life, you will get what you want in life."

Whatever it is, figure it out today. It will change your life forever and make every day a great day no matter how bad life seems to get. Stop blaming others for where you are in life. Don't give your circumstances or other people control over your emotions or life. Take control of your PURPOSE today.

APPLICATION TO MAXIMIZE YOUR DASH

What keeps you from defining your purpose in life?

What brings the most meaning to your life?

What people do you love to serve?

What cause do you feel deeply connected to, and want to help?

What life experiences have you had that have prepared you to serve?

What gifts and talents do you possess that could help others?

ACTION STEP TO MAXIMIZE YOUR DASH

Write down your purpose in life.

CHAPTER 9

DISCOVER YOUR PASSION

"It doesn't matter what age you are, what stage of life you are in, or how much money you have, EVERYONE has a passion burning inside of their soul."

One thing I know in life is that people love dealing with exciting people. Exciting isn't about jumping up and down, screaming, and having crazy emotions all the time. Excitement is about a life giving off positive energy, that makes people feel good about themselves. In life, you either build people up, or you tear them down. People with energy and passion penetrate the hearts and souls of others. They bring life to sad people. They give life to those not feeling worthy. If you want people to encourage your passion, discovering and living out your passion is a must.

Every day people wake up in a fog. They are people who are simply going through the motions of life, waiting on something to trigger their inner soul and passion…to motivate them to step into everything that life has to offer them. They are waiting to find the right person…waiting to have enough money to have a child…waiting on the right job… waiting for the kids to grow up so they can date one another again…waiting on the right time to retire…waiting, waiting, waiting… Waiting on WHAT?

All the while YOU are waiting, your life is passing YOU by. You wake up one day, look back, and realize that you have just wasted two years, five years, and sometimes more…waiting. Waiting for WHAT? What are you waiting on?

You go through life each day doing the same mundane tasks. You get up…if you have kids, you get the kids off to school…if you don't, you sleep a little later…you go to work…you come home…you do chores around the house… you eat dinner…you go to bed…you get up, and repeat. This mundane activity over time ultimately drives you crazy. One day, you wake up years later, and feel like you have wasted years of your life with no passionate energy that gives LIFE to your life. Your Dash feels empty.

So many couples lose their marriage because they become bored with one another. This is how affairs start. Two married people, in boring marriages, innocently start talking about their boring lives, and next thing you know, they're sharing things that bond them emotionally. That emotion connects them in a way, that at some point, drives them to cross the line in their marriages. Why? …because of the intense excitement of their bond. Don't wait until the kids grow up. That's 18 to 25 long years or more. If you are married, you and your spouse need to find your individual passions in life and start living them out around one another. That alone will create more excitement than you could ever imagine. There is something sexy and exciting about engaging a person to talk about their passions and watching them in pursuit of them. They become interesting and their energy flows into your soul. Don't let someone else capture your spouse or significant other's smile with their life's passion. Discover yours and capture their heart with it...all over again.

Many people switch jobs because it is no longer challenging. It pays well. You could do it in your sleep, yet you want to move to another job for a new challenge. Why? You have been blessed with a job that you can do in your sleep because you are excellent at it, and because you do it well, you are off at a reasonable hour and don't carry the stress of work home. You are FREE to enjoy everything else life has to offer you. Don't let being challenged at work be your sole purpose for existence in life. Discover your passion outside of work and make that your challenge. Be challenged to engage your friends. Be challenged to engage your children. Be challenged to engage and connect with your spouse.

It doesn't matter what age you are, what stage of life you are in, or how much money you have, EVERYONE has a passion burning inside of their soul. It's the cause, group of people, or thing, that gets your blood flowing…it drives your emotions. Your passion is that place where, if you could be a part of it and not get paid, you would do it in a heartbeat. However, if you could get paid to do it, how cool would that be! For some, their passion is children…for others it's animals…others it's the environment… others it's cancer, heart disease, or the elderly. What's yours?

My passion is people. I love people. It fits right into my purpose discussed in the previous chapter. For over twenty years I've worked in executive management for non-profit trade associations. One of the most amazing reasons I love working for an association is that it provides me an open forum to make a difference in people's lives. It allows me the opportunity to help them transform from going nowhere in life, to heading in the direction of their dreams… from feeling pain, to feeling the pleasure and excitement of living out their passions…from being angry and hurt, to being happy and whole…from feeling like they aren't worth much, to knowing they are worth it all.

Living your passion isn't about waiting until you have the time to pursue or finance it. It is about discovering what it is and starting in the pursuit of it…NOW…like TODAY!

I can remember when I got to live out my passion at an extremely high level. Granted, I have lived out my passion for the last 20 years as CEO of three different non-profits, but the second one is an amazing story of making a decision to start living out my passion.

It was 2001, and I had just left my first trade association in Orlando, Florida to move to Jacksonville, so I could be near my two children, who had moved there a few years earlier through their mom's second marriage. I had started an online fundraising business circled around online auctions, and it was beginning to build momentum when 9-11 happened. As with many small businesses, mine was a casualty of 9-11, in that my business model depended on companies to donate items for online auctions to benefit non-profits. Once 9-11 occurred, companies wanted to give most of their charitable contributions towards the 9-11 cause, and my business went by the wayside.

With a "never give up" attitude, and needing a job, I proceeded to market myself around Jacksonville, Florida for CEO jobs in local non-profits. It's what I knew best and was very good at it. Over the span of a year, I interviewed with numerous companies. Eight times I made it through hundreds of applications, numerous interviews, and made it to the final two. Eight times that happened! All eight times they went with the other candidate. I couldn't believe it. I was told each time that the other person had an intangible edge that they felt like they needed to go with.

The one lesson I want to share with you right here is, "Passion breeds perseverance." When you are passionate about who you are and what you want to do in life, nothing can get in your way. It is just a matter of time before everything lines up, and BAM, you are living it out.

My decision to take the leap to pursue my passion on another level came on the front porch of a friend's house. The year before I moved to Jacksonville, I attended a weekly gathering of over 1,000 single adults called *Orlando Metro*. It was a weekly event where single adults could come into a healthy environment, listen to an amazing live band, hear a life-giving message on relationship skills, and meet new friends. Over the year I attended, my life swelled with joy, my network of positive friends grew by ten-fold, and my life was transformed. When I moved to Jacksonville, I put a two-page executive summary together for an *Orlando Metro* concept in Jacksonville, called *Jax Metro Live*. That executive summary sat on my desk until after I had been passed over for a CEO job for the eighth time. That's right…eight times.

I was on the front porch with a friend, enjoying a chilled beverage, on the night of coming up short for the eighth time for a major position. My friend and I were chatting and laughing about how crazy it was for me to make it past hundreds of applicants, multiple interviews, only to come up the number two choice eight times. That's got to be a record somewhere.

My friend looked at me at one point, knowing my internal desire for my *Jax Metro Live* concept, and said, "Tom, instead of interviewing people for a job, why don't you interview people for money to start *Jax Metro Live?*" My heart started pumping, my adrenaline started running, and my mind started racing. I couldn't believe what he had just proposed to me. I immediately said, "That is an amazing idea!" That night I lived out and practiced what I preach to everyone...sometimes you just have to make a choice to pursue your passion and run after it, so I did.

I immediately started networking around Jacksonville to find the movers, shakers, and funders for people like me with an idea that could change people's lives. Within a few months, I had a major contribution from a well-known businessman for startup costs and another one hosted a fundraising dinner for me. I had a major facility, with state-of-the-art meeting space offer to host the weekly event for free, a very talented band came on board, and a nationally known speaker on relationship skills signed with us to help us reach the singles community in Jacksonville. All of this happened within a five-month span. It was crazy how everything we needed just came to me.

When *Jax Metro Live* hosted its first event, it drew in over 300 people. By week three, we had over 600 people coming every Thursday night to hear amazing live music, life-giving talks, and networking with others through the challenges and opportunities in life. It was powerful. I was living my purpose and passion every day...engaging the lives of thousands of people from as far as an hour away, to help them know that there was more to life than their pain and their past. Over the three-year period of Jax Metro Live, we saw people who were running a bad path of life on drugs, alcohol, bad decisions, and horrible pasts, find purpose in their life, self-worth, and a path to living the ultimate life. Every email or conversation I had with people about their changed life made my heart swell with joy.

I share that story to illustrate that your passion is just a choice away. It's one step away from becoming a reality for you. That is not to say that you need to quit your job or run off on some tangent in life. You need to be smart about your choices, but you could be closer than you think to embarking on the journey of living out your passion.

I've been working in association management since February 20, 1995. I remember it like it was yesterday. Every day has been an incredible journey. It hasn't come without its set of challenging moments, but when your purpose is in place and you are serving in your area of passion, challenges are always seen as opportunities, not obstacles.

If purpose gives you a direction, then passion is what defines you. It's what gives you energy every day because you are working on, or serving in, an area that creates an emotional excitement in your life. What you are passionate about is what causes you to take ACTION and energizes your life. My questions to you, with regards to discovering your passion, are:

- What are you accomplishing with your life?
- What gets your blood boiling?
- What do you care about?
- What people would you like to serve/help?
- What would you do if money were no object?
- What would get you excited every day to get out of

bed?
- Who would you help every day for no pay, just because you love it?
- What is your hobby?

Some of mine are: I LOVE playing drums...it drives my emotional high. I LOVE dancing to 70's and 80's music...it makes me feel good physically. I LOVE speaking to groups of people on life and association management. I LOVE seeing them write down action steps to help them transform their lives. I LOVE making videos that share stories of how associations are making a difference in people's lives. Bottom line...I LOVE PEOPLE, and I LOVE HELPING THEM achieve success.

If you are like me, you like to see an example of what things look like, especially when you are looking to design your own plan of action from scratch. For your reference, here is what my purpose and passion statement looks like:

Tom's Purpose Statement

My purpose is to engage people in conversation, network with people, and connect them, helping them reach their maximum potential, and living a deeper and more rewarding life.

Tom's Life Passion:

Seeing people go from, "I'm struggling", to "I LOVE my LIFE!"

Make a commitment today to design your Life Purpose and Passion Statements and live them out. Someone out there needs your purpose and passion in their challenging life. You won't regret making the choice and taking that step.

APPLICATON TO MAXIMIZING YOUR DASH

What keeps you from pursuing your passion in life?

What is the one cause you have a passion for?

What people would you love to help?

If you were guaranteed a comfortable lifestyle, what would you do that would feed your soul and make you feel the most rewarded?

ACTION STEPS TO MAXIMIZING YOUR DASH

Write down you Purpose statement:

Write down your passion statement:

Write down three steps that you must take to begin to live out your passion in life:

1)

2)

3)

CHAPTER 10

DECIDING YOUR PRINCIPLES

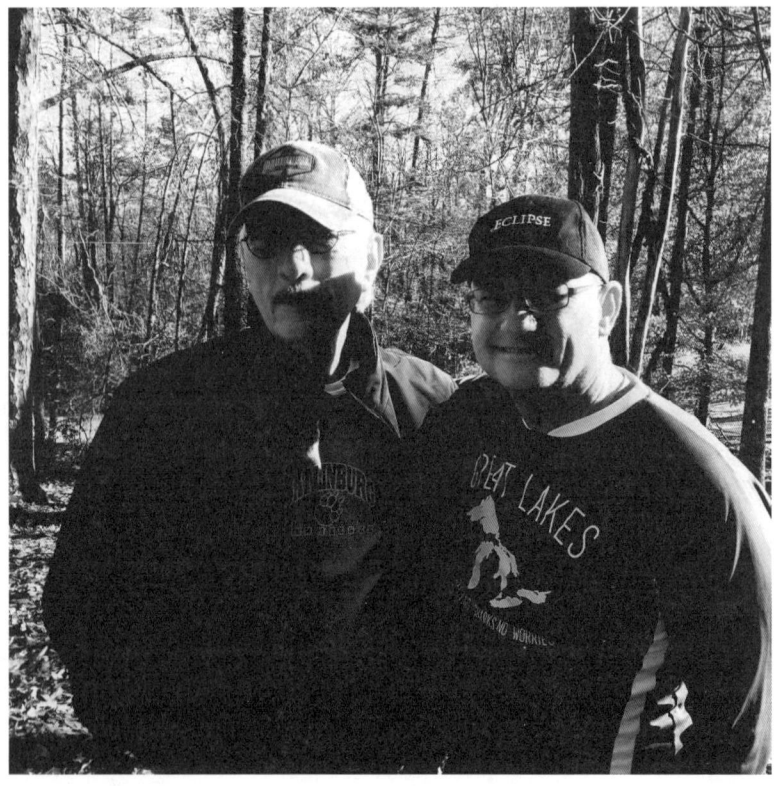

"Your principles will be what you are remembered for. It's what you stand for, and the legacy that you will leave behind with your kids and grandkids."

Now that you have engaged your thoughts about defining your Purpose and discovering your Passion, the third element to maximizing Your Dash is to decide what Principles you are going to live your life by.

Webster's dictionary defines Principles as: *a fundamen-*

tal, primary, or general law or truth from which others are derived, a fundamental doctrine, a personal or specific basis of conduct or management, or a guiding sense of the requirements and obligations of right conduct.

The key words in the definition are: truth, personal, conduct, guiding, requirements, and right conduct.

You see, your principles are what guide your conduct, your heart, and your beliefs, which speak to your character and integrity. Principles are the road map of how you will go about accomplishing anything in your life. They will determine the types of people you will surround yourself with, the type of actions you will take, and how you make key decisions. More importantly, it will drive whether or not people want to interact, do business with, and associate with you.

When people look at you, what kind of principles do they see in you? When you are walking towards people in your company, what are they thinking about you as you approach? How do you make people feel as you approach them, without even saying a word?

The principles people see in you, drive what they think about you, and how willing they are to help, trust, and associate with you. If people do not think you are trustworthy, you will have a hard time finding people willing to help you. If people see you as a "user of people", you won't find people willing to step out on a limb for you. If people don't see you as a hard worker, they will not be willing to jump on your team and work hard for you.

The key Principles in your life can be discovered by asking yourself:

- Who are my biggest influences?
- What do I believe in the areas of trust, truth, honesty, ethics, integrity, work ethic, and friendships?
- What do I expect from other people?

- What are people's perceptions of me?
- Do my actions match up with my beliefs and what I say?
- Am I doing the right things when no one's watching?
- Who do I go to for advice when I'm in need of guidance?
- What books do I read to strengthen what I believe in life?

One of the most comforting emotions in life is the confidence you have when someone says something, and you can take what they say to the bank, because their actions always match their words. It breeds confidence in the workplace as a leader, in relationships as a partner, in children as a parent, and especially in friendships.

I've seen one lie destroy a ten-year friendship. I've seen people fired over dishonesty. We have all seen marriages broken over mistrust. Your Principles dictate how everything takes place in your life. The question you should be asking yourself is, "do your Principles align with your Purpose and Passion?"

When it comes to my Principles, I take them from the Bible. The Bible has over 2,000 years of proven truths and life skills for every aspect of your life in relationships, parenting, friendships, how to deal with difficult circumstances, and even business relationships.

When seeking where to draw your Principles from, you need to make sure their foundation will move your life in a positive direction that you desire. Look at the lives of the people who live by those principles, and ask yourself, "Do the principles they live by and stand for take them in a positive direction in life?" If the answer is no, then you need to steer clear of those principles. Having a wrong set of guiding principles can ensure your obituary will suck because you will be running uphill for many of life's big moments.

Whether you are a spiritual person or not, it is critical in your life to define where you get your principles from, define them, study them, practice them, and then live them out.

Over my life, I have developed some sound principles that have helped me in every aspect of my life that I believe you would want to pay attention to. These will help you miss some of the potholes in the road of life per se. The following are my top twelve key principles that have helped me persevere, obtain the ultimate life, and make sure my obituary won't suck:

Failure Is Not an Option

If "quit" is in your vocabulary, you will always come up short in life in any area. Remember, one of the keys we have already discussed is the ability to persevere. Whether it's business, marriage, college, or any other aspect of life, you need to know that if you choose the right purpose, path, and people for your decision, you will succeed. Remember, achieving great things in life are never easy. They usually come with a bumpy road, unexpected twists and turns, as well as, some push back. Almost every idea ever created was not created just by the person who patented it or actually pulled it off. Most every idea was thought of previously by many people, however, only one person, or a small group of like-minded people, pulled it off because of their tenacity, perseverance, and a desire not to fail. If you want to be on stage, you need to know you belong on that stage. If you want a certain degree in college or a certain job, you need to know you "own" that degree or job. If you want to climb Mount Everest, you need to know you can "own" that mountain. So many quitters were five minutes, or one more key decision away, from having their desires and dreams come true…but they stopped short and walked away.

I love a quote in the movie *A League of Their Own*, a movie about the development of a professional women's baseball league back during war times. As the demands of being a full-time baseball player got tough on Dottie (played by Geena Davis) she wanted to quit. As she was walking to get in her car with her husband, who had just returned from the war, the team manager, Jimmy (played by Tom Hanks) confronted her to ask her why she was quitting. She said, "It got hard and became tough." Jimmy said something I have never forgotten. He said to Dottie, "Did you think it was going to be easy? If it were easy, everyone would be doing it. It's supposed to be hard. The hard is what makes it GOOD."

Anything worth achieving is not going to be a cake-walk. However, your perseverance will feel incredible when you accomplish your goal, and your character and strength to overcome obstacles will grow to all time levels. Don't ever quit on your dreams, desires, and passions…you could be one decision away from all of them coming true.

Let Go of Your Past

(I discuss this in greater detail later.) This Principle is so huge for everyone, yet so many people never accomplish any of their dreams in life because of the people and experiences in their past. Some allow the past to keep them down. Others use the past as a motivator to excel. If there is someone you need to forgive to set yourself free of the past, I encourage you to do it today. If there is something you need to say to your parents to move on…do it today. If there is an experience you have buried in your soul that you need to confront, or something that needs to be said to someone…figure out how to do it soon. People lose decades of their life holding on to their past, and it just isn't worth it. Do whatever it takes to heal your past. Seek a professional counselor, a mentor, or a life coach. Sometimes just talking it out is enough to get it out of your soul. I've personally seen the past strip some people close to me, of as much as 25 years of their life before they finally said, "I don't want to live like that any longer."

What is in your past that is holding you back? An abusive parent? A bad relationship? Friends who have betrayed you? Addiction? Whatever it is, get it out starting today! Get help, take action, set goals, and then GO FOR YOUR DREAMS!

Treat Others "First" How You Would Like to Be Treated

In my lifetime, I have found that the people you surround yourself with, treat you how you have treated them first. If you continually treat someone with love, respect, and decency, and they do not do the same to you, then they have something going on within their own life, and they are never going to be someone who helps Your Dash. They will always be a negative force in your life that tears down your spirit and will easily make your obituary suck. Should you ignore them and never hang with them? ...of course not. I have many people I hang with occasionally, who are in this frame of mind, but they are not part of MY PEOPLE that I know and can count on to be fans and be a proactive part of my life. I still treat them with respect, love, and decency when I'm with them, but I don't let them waste my valuable time with their negativity, and you shouldn't either. To maximize

Your Dash, you must minimize the time wasters and drama builders in your life.

Be the Change

I'm sure you have heard the saying many times, "If you continue to do things the way they have always been done, and expect different results in your life, then you are going to drive yourself crazy.

Because of technology, everything in life changes at such a rapid speed. To be successful in both personal and business life, it is critical that you embrace change; some change will be an exciting fad, others will be permanent. You need to be able to discern between the two, so you can make shifts to react to permanent change. Making these shifts will help you to enhance your quality of life and maximize your business opportunities. Those who thought Facebook, Uber, and Zillow were fads, are now operating at a disadvantage in business, because they aren't taking advantage of technology shifts that could help make their life easier, and business more profitable. There are shifts in many areas: like how you can invest, communicating with people, transportation, etc. Change is all around us and happening all the time. If you ignore it, you will fall behind and lose the opportunity to maximize Your Dash and create opportunities, memories, and success in many areas of your life. Later in the chapter on networking, I'm going to share why everyone should be an active user on social media and how it can expand your life and Your Dash.

Managing is About the Process, Leading is About the People

This is a principle that is the most misunderstood principles on my entire list. The key to this principle is understanding that when you are in management, you are in charge of the process…the technical portion of the strategy. You engage in the day-to-day operations, and you are working closely with your people to get things done. If you are in leadership, the key acronym you need to know is "GOOTW." This stands for GET OUT OF THE WAY. If you want to be an effective leader, you need to make sure that you communicate clearly to those that you lead, the "What", and then let your people take care of the "How." If you want your team to maximize their creativity and output, you need to communicate the goals and expectations, then empower them and get out of the way. From there you check in at points in time, to ensure "strategically" that the team is on target. If they are, get out of the way…if they aren't, identify the gap, how to close it…and get out of the way. I have found when you empower your team, give them ownership to use their talents and ideas, your output in anything far surpasses your expectations, instead of you dictating everything.

Don't Judge a Book by Its Cover

Every day you will meet people. Know that each of those people have a past, a personality, a story, and reasons why they may look like they do, act like they do, and think like the do. You may see people with tattoos dressed a certain way, or in a certain financial situation, and make pre-judgments about them. …wrong way to think. Never judge someone until you have had a chance to meet them, talk to them, and get to know their story. Everyone has a story. If they are in the midst of a struggle that is causing their negative outlook on life, you may be the one person who may speak encouraging or empowering words into their life that helps their life take a powerful turn. Many people on the inside are not what you think they are, because of what we see on the outside. What gives us the right to make assumptions about people based on what we see?

I can remember in 1998 I had two of my employees needing to take time off for six to eight weeks for childbirth and back surgery. I really needed someone to help me bridge the eight-week gap at work. I had a number of people I was considering. One of my employees encouraged me to interview her sister, who was a stay-at-home mom for 17 years. My first "judgment" was that since she was a stay-at-home mom, she couldn't possibly fit into our fast-paced business. I decided to forgo my initial judgment and talk to her anyway.

After one interview, I realized that she had all the skill sets that we were looking for. When I listened to what her day was like during the last seventeen years of being an at home mom, she had amazing skill sets in organization, leadership, management, operations, meeting people's needs, and customer service. The bottom line is, I hired her, and she ended up being one of the most effective employees I have ever had. She was so effective that I figured out that the two employees that went on leave had been dishonest with their time, leading me to think that they had a full days' work day in and day out. The new employee proved to me that they only had a half days' work by doing both of their jobs more effectively by herself. Needless to say, she stayed with me long term and the other two found other jobs.

The keys again are to meet, listen, and understand people's stories. Focus more on what they say, and more importantly what they do. Actions and results should match what they say. You would want the same respect.

If You Can't Do the Time, Don't Do the Crime

When I was a baseball player in high school, our coach hated when any of us watched a third strike go by. He would always say, "To be successful in life, you must go down swinging." He disliked us not swinging at the third strike so much, that if you were called out on a third strike, you had to run five laps around our baseball field, which was about one and a quarter miles. If you watched a third strike and tried to lobby for, "it was a bad call," my coach would always say, "Listen, if it's close enough to be called a strike, it's close enough for you to swing at."

I tell that story for you to remember, if you are close enough to be pulled into a bad choice that can have a negative impact on the future of your life, it's close enough for you to be caught and carry some painful consequences. If you want the ultimate quality of life and don't want your obituary to suck, know that cheaters are always found out, people never succeed through using drugs, trying to outsmart the law doesn't pay, and betraying your people will come with heavy consequences. You may live the high life for a while, but when you are found out or exposed, the bottom will fall out...and fast. The pain and expense of your recovery will be immense. My encouragement for you is to live your life right when you come to those forks in the road of a good and bad choice.

That brings to mind a story in my life that I hope every young person takes to heart. I was in my mid teens and I was a pretty compliant kid, but I had a bit of an attitude, a smart mouth, and just didn't always do the things my parents asked me to do around the house. I wasn't a rebellious child off on wild excursions, but I just wasn't an agreeable teenager at times. I was like most teenagers, and thinking that life was about me, not others. Everything came to a halt one day at sixteen, when I mouthed off to my father. He stuck his hand out and asked for my keys to "OUR nice, customized Dodge van" that I had gotten for my sixteenth birthday. I loved that car and had so much fun with it in high school. I looked at him in dismay and I was like, "The keys to OUR car?" You see I thought the car was really mine, but I thought wrong. He said, "Yes, the keys to OUR car. We bought the car. You get to use the car. We get to take away the car for direct disrespect and disobedience." I knew I wasn't going to win this one, so I gave him the keys and had to get rides from my friends for two weeks. My father told me, "When you can learn, and have shown you can treat your parents with respect and decency, you can have your keys back."

Over the next couple of weeks, I did some soul searching, and realized a principle early in life, that changed my life with people: "If you continually piss people off, are naturally non-compliant, and make life tough on them, they will almost always say 'no' to you, and will be unwilling to help you." Read that again and let it sink in, "If you continually piss people off, and make life tough on them, they will almost always say 'no' to you and will be unwilling to help you."

In my room that night, I made a commitment, as a 16-year-old, to do whatever my parents asked. I cleaned my room up. I cut the lawn when needed. I was home by eleven or called before eleven to ask for permission to be out later and made sure they knew whom I would be with. It was all the typical things parents ask of a teenage son or daughter. What immediately started happening was my parents' lives became less stressful, they had more time to enjoy their own life instead of cleaning up after me, and they felt like I respected their house because I kept my part clean. What happened was a huge shift in how they dealt with me.

They began to say, "YES" to almost anything I asked. My trust level with them was off the charts because I was proving to them that I cared about what we had, and I wanted them to enjoy their life, so I wasn't creating unnecessary stress in their lives. Every day I see so many people creating so much unnecessary stress in people's lives because they are just not naturally compliant and pursue the negative in everything.

In life, you have a choice in every area, to be naturally compliant or rebellious. I believe you need to have a compliant attitude with a rebellious streak that feeds your passion… not the other way around. Just know that if you are that person who chooses to always have a rebellious attitude with a streak of compliance, life is going to deliver push back, hard paths to walk to get to your goals, and less people willing to help you be successful. In my opinion, a rebellious spirit is a path to an obituary that will suck because you will always be running uphill in many areas of life. There is nothing wrong with diversity of thought and creativity that goes against a way of thinking, but to rebel in a way that always puts you in the opposition will not lead to an easy life for anyone.

People don't have to like you for you to live the ultimate life…they just need to respect you. When faced with the fork in the road with a decision, weigh the cost of whether it will enhance your life or cause grave consequences. It's your choice every time.

Birds of a Feather Flock Together

When it comes to the people you surround yourself with, make sure they have your best interest at heart, and are going the same direction as you are. I will cover this area in greater detail in a few chapters. The key in this area is whom you surround yourself with.

You Reap What You Sow

This principle is a combination of how you treat others, the choices you make, how you invest your time, and how much you put others before yourself. In life, you really do get what you deserve, as well as, what you put into it. If you work hard, make good choices, operate with a high level of integrity, and treat people with respect and decency, then your life is going to have great things happen. That doesn't mean it will be perfect, or you won't have to deliver a firm hand in certain areas, but people will want to come together and help you.

If you make bad decisions, treat people with a negative or bully mentality, fudge the truth, and look for short cuts, your life is going to be filled with drama, push back, a lot of "No's", and a lack of the "right people" willing to help you.

If you continue to see bad things happen to you in your life, you need to look at my *Path to the Ultimate Life* visual and analyze your decision-making process. Take the time to find three mentors in your life who know your heart, want the best for you, know where you want to go, and consistently confide in them the choices you are faced with to gain their input. The best way to not make bad decisions is to talk to someone who has "been there done that." Mentors can steer you towards a good path to meet your life goals. The key here, is to have people who don't tell you what you want to hear, but people who, knowing all the facts you have given them, will give you open and honest guidance and feedback on which path to take.

Say What You Mean and Mean What You Say

This one is pretty straight forward, but so many people screw this up in life. I've had people tell me about people they thoroughly enjoy working with at any level because when they commit or say something, "you can take it to the bank."

Don't say things to people that you don't mean, and don't commit to things that you don't intend to follow through on. This "double talk" will dilute your effectiveness and dependability factor to everyone around you. People want to know they can count on you...they really do. Don't be the person that people make the comment, "Yeah...he always says that." You always want to be someone that people know that they can count on.

A key in the area of communication is to know that some things are better left unsaid. Once upon a time, I can remember walking into a men's study group that I was a part of years ago. On the white board in the room there were three words that a prior group had been talking about that are important in communication: timing, message, intent. I was like, "I could have used that last night." Not everything has to be said at a specific moment. There is a right time to communicate and say some open and honest things to someone, and there is a wrong time. Make sure that what you want to say to someone has a positive impact on the situation. Have your words move things forward, not backward.

You Get What You Pay For

Cheap breaks. Cheap only works short term. Cheap almost always needs to be fixed by those who provide quality work or products. One day I was driving, and I saw on one side of the road a brake shop that had on their sign, "Brake Jobs: $19.95." Across the street was another brake shop that had on their sign, "We fix $19.95 Brake Jobs." I started laughing when I saw it because it is so true. If you want your obituary to not suck, don't beat everyone up to give you cheap pricing on something. They have a cost associated with doing business, and in ultimately providing the level of service that you demand and need. They need to be able to charge enough to service you with levels of excellence. Now, that doesn't mean that you don't put things out for a bid periodically and be a good shopper...I do it all the time, but I do it to keep my suppliers in check, and to let them know that competition exists. Once I get some competitive quotes back, if some are much lower than my current cost, I'll sit down with my supplier and ask them to share with me why their pricing is higher. They will either match the price with the same service, educate you that you will not get the same high level of service by going to the other company and you stay put, or you move to the new supplier at a lower cost.

The point here is, don't let price drive your decisions. It can end up costing you more money in the long run. With anything in life, whether personal or business buying decisions, make sure you consider quality and service before pricing.

When people know you will not leave them overnight for a cheaper price, they are willing to do way more for you in the service area. Leverage that to your benefit.

Invitations + Time and Money = YES! (Every time)

I will expand on this in a later chapter, but I wanted to mention it here in my list of key principles. I see so many people who miss out on some great experiences because they just say "no" to invitations to experience life. My philosophy has always been, "If I'm invited to do something adventurous in life, and I have the time and the money, I always say, 'YES.'" I've experienced so many spontaneous adventures in my life with friends and family by just saying, "I'm IN!"

I can remember a conference that I attended in the automotive industry in 1998. The hotel was full, and I was able to go because one of our members had a friend who would let me room with him. He was a very successful man in his seventies, who was semi-retired from the business, but he liked to stay connected, so he continued to attend the annual conference. I remember us sitting in the room about to go to bed, when he spoke words into my life that changed my life in this area. He said, "Tom, let me share some life advice with you. I'm now in my seventies. When I was young and healthy, I always said to myself, "When I have the time and money I'm going to do all these fun and exciting adventures in life. Well as you can see, I now have all the time and money I could want, and I can't do any of those fun and exciting things because of my health. Live life in the moment as much as you can." Anyone who is close to me would tell you I have lived that advice out as much as possible.

Don't let life get in the way of you experiencing your bucket list this year. Your health or other life factors could change at any moment and get in the way...experience life NOW! Remember the block exercise in chapter two? Don't wait until a whole series of blocks are wiped out instantly because of some life or health issue. When invited, say, "I'm

In!" This is the #1 life motto to making sure your obituary won't suck.

So, there you have it. Those are my dozen principles that have guided my life. You will see these expanded on throughout the rest of the book. If you are consistently running off course in achieving your purpose, the first place to start is looking at the principles that guide your life, and how those are connected to your decision-making process. Look at your life purpose, your passion statement, and ask yourself, "Is what I believe (My Principles), going to get me to where I want to go?" If the answer is "no", then it's time to rethink your Principles.

APPLICATION TO MAXIMIZING YOUR DASH

Where do you get your life principles from?

How are your principles helping you excel in life?

ACTION STEPS TO MAXIMIZING YOUR DASH

Write down five key principles you want to live your life by:

1)

2)

3)

4)

5)

CHAPTER 11

SETTING YOUR PRIORITIES

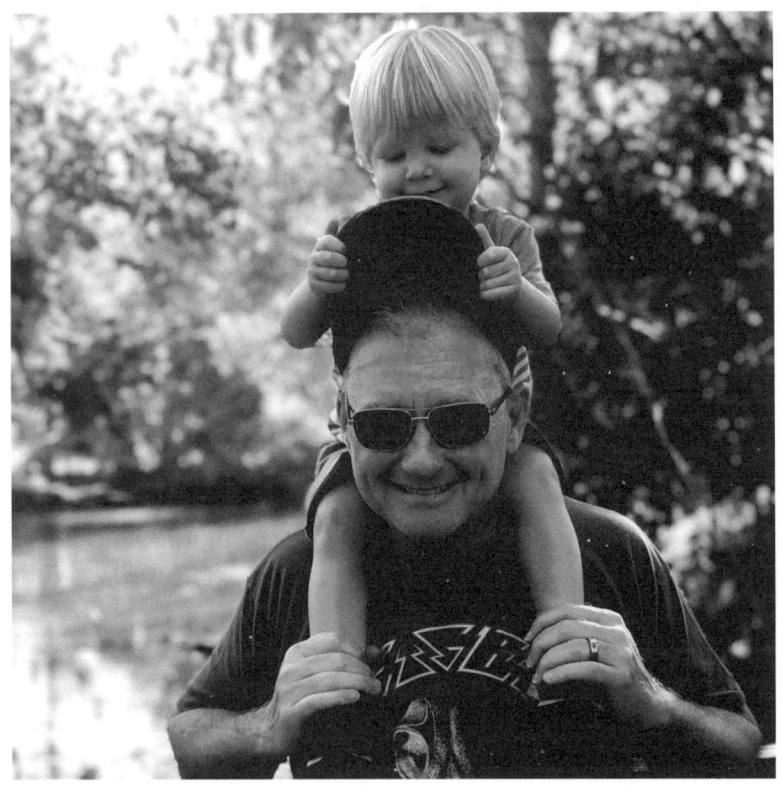

"You can tell a person's priorities by looking in their checkbook and day timer. How a person spends their time and money tells you what their priorities are."

Now that you have defined your PURPOSE, discovered your PASSIONS, decided on your PRINCIPLES, it's time to get your PRIORITIES in order. PRIORITIES are the visual display of your actions, matching up with your words. In a sense, they are where you want to end up at the end of your life. It's what you want the dash to stand for between the dates when you were born and the date you pass on. It's the list of things people say you focused on throughout your life.

A couple of questions to think through at this point are, "Do you know what you want said about you at the end of your life?" Do your actions match up with what you say your priorities are?

I want you to turn back to page 6 and stare at your life in a set of colored boxes. Focus on the boxes that are not colored in. That is what you have left in life…the amount of time you have to make sure your obituary won't suck. If there are a lot of white boxes, you are still young…you have time to shape your priorities in a way that will expand your life opportunities to create the ultimate life for your future. My hope is that if you are under 30, you don't do what so many others do, and wait until you are 40+ to start thinking about why are you here and what your priorities should be. You may think you are all-powerful in your 20s and will live forever, but I have a cousin who woke up one day to his 19-year-old married daughter calling him with what she thought was a painful headache. She was seven months pregnant, and within two hours of that phone call, she was in a coma from a sudden stroke type condition. She lived on life support in a hospital for the next six weeks until the baby was able to be born without complications. The number of people her life reached over the next couple of months, as they kept her alive for the baby to be born, was more than most of us will reach in a lifetime. She was a true blessing, and fortunately had all of her priorities in order at 19. Sadly, she was taken far too early. That could be you at twenty, thirty-two, forty-five, or over sixty. Life can be shortened in a heartbeat. Start NOW, at whatever your age is, get your priorities in alignment with where you want to be, and how you want to be remembered, and watch it create the ultimate quality of life that you desire. At the end of the day, many people's obituaries suck because their priorities were out of whack compared to where their true desires were.

If you are 40+, the clock is ticking and your time to engage life will begin to disappear…quickly. Before Facebook, you never knew so many of your high-school classmates died prematurely due to cancer, unexpected heart attack, or some kind of accident, until you attended one of your class reunions. Now with Facebook and other forms of social media, you hear about it the moment they pass, because someone, somewhere, is posting about it on a social media platform. Think about it…once you get over 40, health becomes more of a serious issue. A change in health should not be the time that you decided to change your priorities. If you wait, you may not have the health to fulfill those priorities.

The point is, if you are a college student, don't live life in a way that when you wake up at 40, you figure out that your priorities were all wrong. If you are over 40, you need to get your priorities in order…NOW. Don't wait until a doctor says the spot on your chest, or the pain in your head, are going to wipe the years out of your life and your time is limited.

When setting your priorities, there are four simple places you need to look to know what your priorities are:
- What do you spend your time doing?
- Where do you spend your money?
- Who do you spend your time with?
- What difference do you want your life to make?

You can tell people all day long the order of your priorities, but if your calendar, checkbook, and the people you hang with say something else, you are in denial about what your priorities are.

It has been said, you can tell a person's priorities and what they believe in by looking in their Day Timer and checkbook...to see where they invest their time, money, and who they spend time with. This is so true. When I speak to groups on leadership and life growth, I have everyone answer the following basic questions:

1. The following are a list of typical life priorities most people have in their life. Put them in the order you feel are important to you from 1 to 10, with 1 being the top priority, and 10 being the least:

- Wife
- Children
- Other Family
- Work
- Faith or Spiritual Beliefs
- Volunteering (church/nonprofit work)
- Friends
- Personal Health
- Education
- Personal Fulfillment

2. If I were to ask your spouse or significant other to rate you on a scale of 1 to 10 on how much quality time you spend with them, how would they rate you? (10 being great, 1 being poor)

3. If I were to ask your children to rate you on a scale of 1 to 10 on how much quality time you spend with them, how would they rate you? (10 being great, 1 being poor)

4. If I were to ask the ten closest people in your life to rate you on a scale of 1 to 10 on how they see you spend your time, how would they rate you? (10 being great, 1 being poor)

5. If I were to ask your professional colleagues or employees to rate you on a scale of 1 to 10 on how they see you spend your time, how would they rate you? (10 being great, 1 being poor)

6. If we asked your spouse, children, friends, or colleagues to put the above list of priorities in order on how they see you spend your time, money, and who you hang out with, would the list change dramatically from yours?

7. If your next general check-up gave you one year to live, would the order of your priorities change dramatically?

These questions make you look your priorities square in the face and get real with them. I'm never amazed at how many times I do this survey with both young and old executives, and they come back with the following:

- How many hours do you work a week: 75
- How would your spouse rate the quality time you spend with them on a scale of 1 to 10: 3
- How would your children rate the quality time you spend with them on a scale of 1 to 10: 4
- What is your top PRIORITY in life: My Family

This simple example illustrates that family is NOT their top priority, but work is. Now don't get me wrong. I know there are times when, in order to provide for the family, that someone must work more than 40 to 50 hours a week to get through tough economic times, starting up a business, or starting a new challenging job. This just shouldn't be the norm long term, for the sake of your health, your family, and your lifestyle.

When it comes to your priorities, most people want to assign their entire family as their number one priority. I believe you need to even have your family broken up in to separate priorities. I want you to think through breaking up your entire family into three different priorities: your spouse, your children, and all other family. I want you to further think about the concept of making your spouse your number one priority, over your children and other family. Yes, over your children. That doesn't mean that your children receive any less love. What it means is you are going to put your relationship with your life partner ahead of your children. It means you are going to covet and protect that relationship, and not allow anything inside that relationship that could tear it apart. The reason many couples separate over time is because they let all types of distractions and people penetrate the one thing that they stood at the altar and committed to… each other. Trust me, if you make your spouse your number one priority, your kids will benefit because your marriage will live long past them going off to college. If you make your children your priority, your marriage and relationship with your spouse will be put on hold, and when your kids are eighteen years old, you won't know each other, and will most likely separate. I see it happen all around me, and that's if you even make it until your kids are eighteen.

I've seen many young couples get married and say that their spouse is their top priority. But when you look close at how they spend their time, they still are spending time out without their spouse, in places that they shouldn't be in, with people they shouldn't be with. Their spouse is not their top priority.

The same thing applies to your money. Many people say their education or family are their top priority when it comes to money, but when you look how they are spending their money, it says something completely different.

If your personal and professional life seems out of kilter, off balance, or is stressing you out, then your priorities are probably out of order and it is time to do some soul searching. I have learned in both my professional and personal life that if your list of PRIORITIES are not in alignment with your PURPOSE, PASSION, and PRINCIPLES, you will experience conflict and frustration in many aspects of your life and relationships, including your family, spouse, children, employees, etc.

It is critical that you have your priorities written down and ask yourself: Do my actions demonstrate that the PRIORITIES I claim, match up with my PURPOSE, PASSION, and PRINCIPLES? If not, it's time to make some changes.

Before you move on to the next chapter, take some time to really analyze your priorities. This is where the rubber meets the road. To help you make some meaningful changes toward getting your priorities in order, speak to those impacted by your priorities the most, and ask them for their input. Once you have collected input from those closest to you, take the time to do the following steps:

- Look at where you are spending your money.
- Look at where you are spending your time.
- Look at who you are spending your time with.
- What difference do you want your life to make?

Does the time and money you are spending, have your personal or professional life headed in the right direction?

Are the people you are spending your time with moving your life forward or causing it to stall?

You own the decisions of how you spend your time, money, and who you hang with. Align your priorities NOW so that they line up in an order that brings you joy, excitement, and fulfillment to your life each and every day.

Investing time to make sure your professional and personal PRIORITIES are in alignment will pay huge dividends in greater bonds with your family and friends, a life that feels more rewarding, and experiences that make you look back and go "WOW!"

Bottom line...let your actions match your words, and you will begin to experience the "Ultimate Life" and make sure your obituary won't suck.

APPLICATION TO MAXIMIZING YOUR DASH

The following are a list of typical priorities most people have in their life. When you look at your calendar, check-book, and people you hang with on a regular basis, put the following priorities in the order from 1 to 10, with 1 being the top priority and 10 being the least. Be real about your order. You will be asked next to put them in the order you would like to see them in.

- Wife
- Children
- Other Family
- Work
- Faith or Spiritual Beliefs
- Volunteering (church/nonprofit work)
- Friends
- Personal Health
- Education
- Personal Fulfillment

How could your priorities change so that they are feed-ing your life full of joy, the life experiences you desire, and a sense of fulfillment?

How would your spouse, children, family, friends, and professional colleagues rate your priorities?

NOW put your priorities in the order that they need to be in to accomplish the things you stated in your PURPOSE,

PASSION, and PRINCIPLES. Put in order of 1 to 10, with 1 being most important and 10 being least important.

- Wife
- Children
- Other Family
- Work
- Faith or Spiritual Beliefs
- Volunteering (church/nonprofit work)
- Friends
- Personal Health
- Education
- Personal Fulfillment

ACTION STEP TO MAXIMIZING YOUR DASH

What is one action item that you need to take, in each of the following areas, to get your priorities in order:

- Calendar:

- Checkbook:

- People you hang out with:

- What difference do I want my life to make:

CHAPTER 12

THE RIGHT PEOPLE

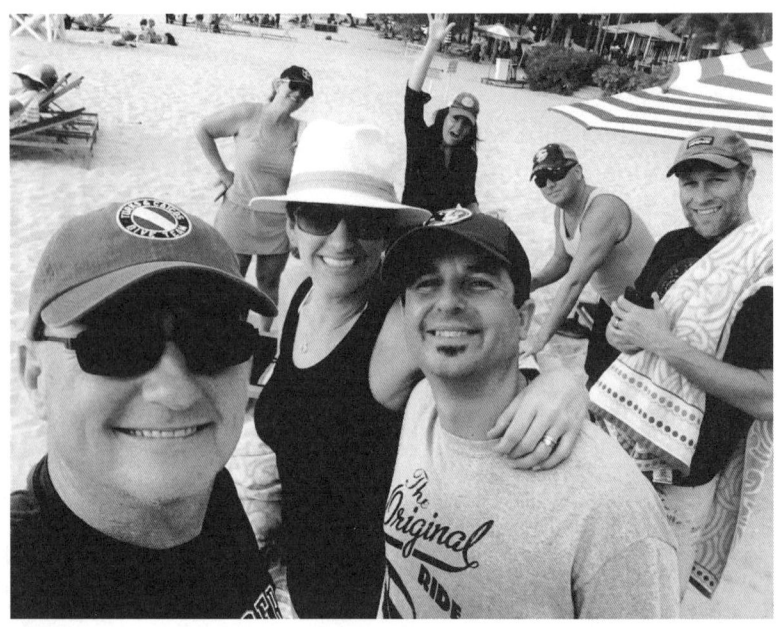

"You will become the people that you hang out with on a regular basis. Good people form good character. Bad people form bad character."

Now that you have defined your PURPOSE, discovered your PASSION, decided your PRINCIPLES, and set your PRIORITIES, it is a MUST that you surround yourself with great people, to engage in life and business successfully. People will be your #1 asset throughout your life. When you need a job, being able to pick up the phone and make two calls to colleagues who have told you, "If you ever make a career change, call me", is powerful. ...Or when you have an employee quit out of nowhere, and you can call three people you know who would love to work for your company. …Or your car breaks down, and you can make a call, and someone will come to help you. Having a large connection of people within your network of life will make life easier, more resourceful, more rewarding, and will definitely make your obituary not suck.

I've learned throughout my entire life that there are a few vital things to remember when you look at the PEOPLE you most closely surround yourself with:

- You never "ARRIVE" and know everything, to where you need no one…we ALL need people.
- You CAN NOT do "life" alone.
- You ARE the PEOPLE you surround yourself with.
- Choose your people WISELY.

YOU NEVER ARRIVE

Have you ever been in a conversation with someone who dominates the conversation? You can't get a word in edgewise, and when you do, even if you prove them wrong, they continue to defend their view? …Or the person who has reached a certain level of success in life, and because of that success, believes they are automatically an expert and the opinions of others don't really matter? These people think they have arrived, and therefore other people, and their thoughts or opinions aren't needed any longer. They couldn't be further from the truth though. No matter how successful you are, there is always someone who knows more, and something new to be learned. To be successful in life, you need to make sure your circle of people includes people smarter and more talented than you are, for two reasons:

- You are challenged to excel and keep growing.
- You have better experts and resources, to help you in many areas of life and business, when needed.

No matter how much you know, how successful or fulfilled you become in life, don't fall for the notion that you have "arrived in life", to where you "know it all" and don't need anyone. Be open, humble, friendly, and embrace as many people around you as possible. There is always someone to learn something from.

DON'T DO LIFE ALONE

So, when you look at your life, do you feel like you are living it alone, or there seems to be no one around helping you? Do you feel like you don't need anyone to help you in life?

People are a MUST in life. It's too busy, chaotic, and tough to try to do it alone. To maximize your success and quality of life, you need to continually grow your people connections in three areas:

People closest to you

These are people around you who know your heart, soul, and mind. They know everything about you and want to help you succeed. These are people you would go to, ask for advice, and spend lots of quality time with.

People who are acquaintances

These are people who you have a friendship with, colleagues in the business world, or anyone else you see occasionally, but aren't close to.

People who know you, but you may not know them

These are people, who somehow have obtained a level of knowledge about you, but you have never personally met them. They could be customers, friends of friends, people who read your blog, etc.

As I stated previously, everyone you meet in life will fall into one of these categories. All of them have an impact on your life at some level, which is why you want to seek to grow in a positive way with each group. Just like you may never know where your resume will end up, you may never know what person in your life will come from out of nowhere and help you in life.

Let me tell you a story about the power of people in your life. So, I had shared with you that I founded JaxMetroLive in 2002, and by the summer of 2005, it was very success-ful at reaching the local community for its cause, but never quite gained enough funding to make it a full-time job for me. I eventually came to a point where I had to consider go-ing back into the corporate world and use my talents there. That was a little scary, given that I had been passed over for eight senior management level jobs just four years earlier. But having a family that I needed to provide for, I made the leap to start looking for my next career. After doing some soul searching, I decided to interview with numerous life insurance and financial planning companies. Insurance and financial planning are where I had my first professional job, so I had some experience. Plus, coming from the non-profit sector of associations, I knew how to speak the language to help non-profit boards provide their executive with a nice retirement package.

I interviewed with four companies and decided on one. I jumped in with a lot of passion and energy, making my prospect calls to close friends, family, and local non-profits. One of my phone calls was to a local trade association CEO that I had met ten years earlier, at some association meet-ings. We got to know each other over a couple of years, but he stopped coming to the meetings and I never saw him after that. As a former colleague, I reached out to him to discuss his financial plan, hoping that he might be able to introduce me to some CEO colleagues to help with their financial plans once I had proven myself with his plan. I left a message for him and never thought much about it.

A couple of weeks later I got a call from him. I asked him to go to lunch, which he agreed to. Before I left the call, he asked me what I thought about getting back into the association management field, and I told him that I thought about it on occasion, but gave no serious considerations, given there weren't many of those types of jobs in my hometown. I told him I had some good things moving with some new clients, and thought financial planning was going to be great for my future.

The next week, we met for lunch. We talked about a lot of things including his plan, what his goals were at retirement, and how much longer he planned to work. As I was talking with him, he kept asking me certain questions about myself and my future. Mentally, I began to think, "it sounds like he is interviewing me to come work for him." After I asked him a few more questions, I couldn't take it any longer. I asked him straight up, "It sounds like you're interviewing me to come work for you. What's up with that?"

He laughed and said, "Tom, I am interviewing you to come work for me." He went on to explain that the number two person in his company did not have the skill set and strengths to lead the association into the future, once he retired. When he discovered that he would need to look for someone else, he began to think of who he could hire to work for him for two years, to learn everything, then take over as CEO. He knew I lived in Jacksonville, and he said to me, "I didn't think I would have to look any further than Tom Morrison, so that's why I called you." I asked him why he felt so strongly that I was "the person" to lead their association into the future. He said, "I remember being in the meetings with you ten years ago, and you were the person who always had the bright fresh ideas and call to action. You were the one with the energy and passion that caught everyone's attention. That's what we need from someone to move our association into the future…someone who can light a fire in our industry. I think that person is you."

Inside I'm thinking, "Wow, this is amazing. I haven't seen him in over eight years and he wants to hire me based on the impression that I left him with over eight years ago." It taught me a valuable lesson…to always leave a good impression with everyone you meet. First impressions are important, but lasting impressions stay with people.

YOU ARE WHO YOU SURROUND YOURSELF WITH

This section is so crucial for you to understand. We are all built for relationships. We want to connect and bond. We want to gain acceptance from our peers and friends. So much so, that we will, in some cases, compromise our principles, what we believe, and even our body to gain their acceptance.

What I've experienced in life, is the people you hang with on a regular basis, will begin to influence your character and the perceptions that other people have of you. I always tell other professionals when they are out with clients or colleagues, be aware of where you are, who you are with, and who could be watching. If you land in the wrong crowd on a regular basis, people will begin to associate you with that crowd, whether good or bad. You may even begin to pick up their bad life habits, whether personal or professional.

Compromising yourself can happen so subtly that you don't even know it right away. I learned this at an early age. It was 1979, I was 15 years old, and a Sophomore in high school. I had gotten my first job as a lawn maintenance guy at an apartment complex. I worked with my uncle and cousin, and we took great pride in making sure the tenants had the best-looking grounds. One day, a new guy started. He seemed pretty cool and friendly. We had a good time while we worked and got along well. However, I noticed that he would take off for a break ten minutes early, stay later on breaks, and walk the long way back after lunchtime. He would almost waste the entire last half hour of each day doing nothing. He could look busy, but he really wasn't committed to the same level of service to the lawn maintenance area as my cousin and I were. But because we got along, I didn't think anything of it at first. When he left for break, I would go with him. I would stay later than normal on lunch break. The next thing I know, I'm doing the same thing that he is. I was wasting at least an hour a day trying to not work very hard. It only took one talk from the foreman, my uncle, to get me back on track to providing an excellence in my work ethic, which I prided myself in. I quickly realized that I was compromising my work ethic, and my reputation, just to gain a new friend and be accepted.

Needless to say, the new guy was soon let go because he didn't have the level of work ethic that we demanded at the company. That could have been me. The people you hang out with on a regular basis will rub off on you. You get to decide what kind of character is going to rub off on you… make good choices.

CHOOSE PEOPLE WISELY

As my examples in this section show, people you hang with on a regular basis will be a positive or negative impact on your life, so CHOOSE THEM WISELY.

The people you surround yourself with don't have to have the same purpose, passion, principles, or priorities as you, but they do need to be aligned with your character, integrity, and goals.

If you want to be an "A" student in school and you are hanging with "C" students, you will end up being a "C" student. If drugs aren't your thing, and you hang with friends who do drugs, you eventually risk compromising your ethics and doing drugs. If you want to have a thriving successful business and you hang out with owners who are continually struggling in business, you will never thrive, but only survive. If you want to be the top sales person in your company, you don't hang and learn from those who just want to make the minimum production goals.

If you want to succeed in life and achieve the quality of life that I'm sharing about in this book, you need to NOT spend all your time with people who have no life plan, live in daily drama, and blame everyone else for their lot in life. If you do, then you will eventually do the same and your obituary will not be what you want.

When you choose who you hang with on a regular basis, both personally and professionally, make sure to get to know who they are, what they want out of life, what they are committed to, and who they hang with. This will give you a good sense of their principles, purpose, passion, and priorities, so you can make sure they are headed the same direction as your life is.

The key is to surround yourself with people who challenge you to grow, who are not afraid to tell you what you need to hear, who ask the hard questions, who are there when you need them, and most importantly, who encourage you on your life journey.

When choosing whom to surround yourself with, you also need to make sure they have good character and integrity. A person of character and integrity is defined as someone whose beliefs and behaviors are in direct alignment with their purpose in life. They say what they mean and mean what they say.

Choose people who are better than you are. Think about it...if you want to improve your golf game, you don't ask someone who shoots ten strokes worse than you how to improve your game. You ask someone who is shooting ten strokes better than you. The same holds true in business and life.

The greatest leaders, business owners, and successful people in life, surround themselves with a team of people who will help them to achieve their goals. When you look at your goals in life, are the people you are surrounding yourself with having a positive or negative impact on you achieving your goals? If they are having a negative impact, or holding you back, you need to make a serious change in who you spend your time with. This doesn't mean you alienate the negative people from your life. You can still have a bond with them, and you can help to encourage their life to be better, but if you are going to excel in life and reach the goals you want, then you need to expand your network of people who will positively help your life to grow every day, and who are moving in the same direction as you are.

Step out of your comfort zone. Look at your PURPOSE, PASSIONS, PRINCIPLES, and PRIORITIES, and start assembling the network of PEOPLE that can help you achieve excellence, excitement, and success.

Do it TODAY and make today the START OF THE REST OF YOUR LIFE!

APPLICATION TO MAXIMIZE YOUR DASH

How do you feel the people in your life help you to be fulfilled in life?

Describe the people you feel are holding you back and what you need to do to correct that?

What would you like to change about the group of people who are in your life the most?

What groups of people could you begin to join who will help you to meet others who are headed in the same life direction as you?

ACTION STEP TO MAXIMIZE YOUR DASH

Write down three action steps you are going to take in the next 30 days to improve the types of people who are in your life on a regular basis?

1)

2)

3)

CHAPTER 13

GETTING PAST YOUR PAST

"As long as your past is in front of you, you will never achieve the quality of life that you want. You must put your past in the past and never look back."

Let's face it, many people know their PURPOSE and PASSIONS, have their PRIORITIES in order, have solid PRINCIPLES, and are surrounded with great PEOPLE, and still never achieve their maximum potential because of one thing: their PAST.

In today's world, there is a lot of hurt and pain in individuals. That pain leads to fear, low self-esteem, lack of confidence, hesitation, and an unwillingness to take risks. All of these are huge obstacles to people living the ultimate life.

Many people have pain in their life from divorce, abuse, bad relationships with their father, mother, boyfriends, girlfriends, being betrayed by a business partner, or just life experiences. Too many things in your past give subconscious control of your emotions over to those who have hurt you in your life. Because of that hurt, you never move forward and achieve all the potential and excitement you desire in your life.

I can remember my divorce that happened in my early 30s. It happened because she fell in love with another man after six years of marriage. It wasn't meant to happen. It just happened. We were a young couple, with two kids, and I wasn't seeking to be all I was meant to be. This brought to life a great saying I once read on Facebook, "Never give someone else the opportunity to make your spouse smile."

The funny thing was, I can remember her standing in our bedroom doorway telling me that I'm worth more than what I'm making. I needed to go out and stake my claim in the world, to build a solid future for our family. She would tell me that I was destined to do something really special in life. As with many young men, I listened, and let it go in one ear and out the other, and it opened the door for another man to make her smile.

She wasn't asking me to win the lotto or make the next rich discovery. She just wanted me to grow into the man I was meant to be for our family. I thought I was doing the best I could, but looking back, I wasn't. I was content just making our bills, playing with the kids, and playing husband. By the way, instead of making more money, I was financing our lifestyle on credit cards. To make a long story short, without all of the gory details, we ended up divorced and I assumed the mounds of credit card debt that I had allowed us to accumulate. The divorce drove a deep wedge in my soul. I never thought I would be divorced. I was now separated from my kids. It was a bad feeling, and I know many reading this book have been there too.

Within a year of the divorce, she married the man she had fallen in love with and moved our kids with her to Jacksonville. That intensified the pain even more, because I adored my children like no other father. I loved being their dad, and now I couldn't just drive over, pick them up, and take them out to the movies or the park. We had to really live the every-other-weekend life, meeting halfway between Orlando and Jacksonville to do the exchange.

Over the next two years, I had this internal anger that just sat in a black box in my soul. It never showed its head publically, and you would never know that there was any pain going on inside of me if you were close to me. God was working on me slowly in the healing process, but the internal anger was there. It kept me up at night. It made me second guess everything I had ever done. It made me think twice about opening my heart up to anyone else ever again. Plus, paying off $36,000 in credit card debt at 18% further intensified the pain.

The bad part about your past, is that it will suck the life out of you if you let it. It will haunt you. It will keep you down. It will make you feel like you aren't worth anything.

The good part about your past, and what I learned from my first divorce, is that good can overcome your past if you just let it. Your past mistakes are your opportunities to learn how to do things differently in the future and to persevere. Your life doesn't end when bad things happen, that's when life begins. The biggest lessons that I took away from that time in my life are:

- Moving past the past is oftentimes a choice.
- If you are going to be all that you can be, you MUST forgive those who have wronged you.

When I looked at what took place in many other divorces, I saw hate, manipulation, and stress. Two things that I didn't want to teach my children in this process were how to hate and manipulate. I wanted my kids to learn how to excel and love in a time when many feel you should be at your worst.

I began to make a choice to get past my past. I made a choice to not argue with their mom in front of them. I made a choice to not talk bad about her in front of them. I made a choice to treat them with decency when we were all together. I made choices to not let my circumstances control my life. I was determined to rise above them because I KNEW that if I was going to heal sooner, rather than later, and take my life to a new positive level, I had to get the past out from in front of me. So, I made a choice.

The second step I mentioned was forgiveness. You know, it really is true, that time has a way of healing wounds. I can remember the day like it was yesterday. It was Easter Sunday and God had been pulling at my heart to do what many never have the strength and nerve to do...forgive my first wife and her husband for their affair. I couldn't help but think that I needed to do it. I had this internal box of anger that wanted to get out, even though I wouldn't let it control my life it was still there. I remember dropping my kids off to them after Easter service, and then driving away. As I drove away, my heart was pulling me back to return and forgive, in person, for all that happened in the past. I wanted to make a choice to pull out the black box of anger in my soul and throw it away. I wanted to be free of the anger, and I didn't want it controlling even one percent of my life. So, I turned around, and asked them to meet me in the driveway of the house to talk. They had no idea what I wanted to say. I proceeded to thank them for being awesome parents to our children. We all know what hangs over us from the past, and I didn't want those circumstances to rule our lives any longer. I wanted to cast out all the guilt, shame, anger, and negativity in our lives that were associated with the past. I told them that I loved them both and I forgave them for everything that took place in our life. I hugged them both and left to celebrate Easter Sunday.

FREEDOM! FREEDOM! FREEDOM! You can't believe the weight off my chest that day. I could move on with life 100% without any thought of the past in my life holding me back. That moment empowered me to be all I could be. It strengthened my soul allowing my life to climb to new levels emotionally and relationally.

Today, my children's mother, her husband, and I are great friends; we live a life free of hate and full of love and joy. More importantly, our kids didn't learn how to hate, they learned how to love. They learned how to make a choice to forgive.

So, what's in your past? What is holding you back? Who do you need to reach out to and have a discussion, to say things you have always wanted to say?

You need to eliminate the negativity of your past. You need to eliminate time-wasters from your life. You need to know that you were put here for a PURPOSE and PEOPLE to serve. Don't let your past and negative people drown your dreams. Eliminate them and pursue your dreams with all your might.

As I conclude this chapter, there is a third lesson that I

learned beyond making a choice to let the past go and for-give. It was to find someone, or a group of people, that will allow you to "empty the bucket" on them. When life deals you a significant blow, all these emotions and thoughts start filling up your brain and your soul. It's like a balloon filling up with air. If you don't let some of the air out at some point, that baby is going to explode! The last thing you need to do is to explode in the wrong place. Find someone, or a small group of people, who know your circumstances, know who you are at your core, and have your best interest at heart. Meet with them periodically to just share what you're think-ing. Get it out…get the anger out…get the hurt out. Once it's all out, then talk about what you need to do to recover and move forward.

For some, you may need a professional counselor to work through your issues. Don't be ashamed to see a coun-selor, they are professionals at helping people to move from pain to pleasure…from hate to love…and addiction to re-covery. Find one and start healing today.

In order for you to experience a life of freedom, and to maximize your potential, you must let your past go. You must turn from looking backwards, so that you can put fo-cus on your future. When it comes to experiencing the fun, excitement, opportunities, and freedom that life has to offer, your past is like a huge bag of rocks weighing you down.

Letting your past go, means dealing with your unfinished business. Unfinished business means facing your past. This means having the discussion with whomever was involved, to reconcile the issue, and most importantly FORGIVING whoever wronged you.

Forgiveness is the most important part of this process. Remember, forgiveness is not about letting someone off the hook. It's about unstrapping the bag of rocks on your back with all the pain, and letting it go. Let your past be a set of lessons for a brighter future, not a set of obstacles that break you down and keep you from your future. To forgive, you don't even have to talk to the person, you can simply write them a letter, an email, or just in your mind have that conversation with yourself and forgive the other person.

From there...you walk forward in FREEDOM, with a renewed feeling of joy, excitement, and optimism.

If you have a desire to experience the ultimate life, do whatever it takes to wipe away the pain of the past. Let today start the rest of YOUR LIFE. Let the pain of the past go and I promise your obituary will not suck. Your future awaits you!

APPLICATION TO MAXIMIZE YOUR DASH

What is in your past that you feel is holding you back from experiencing all that life has to offer you?

Who do you feel has wronged you in a way that is holding you back from being all you can be in life?

What would you want to say to each of these people?

ACTION STEPS TO MAXIMIZE YOUR DASH

What choices do you need to make, starting today, to help you let go of your past?

Who are you going to forgive this week, so you can be free from your past?

Who are you going to ask to let you "empty the bucket" every now and then, to get the negative things off your chest and make positive steps in your life?

CHAPTER 14

PLANNING YOUR PATH

"You need to live out your life with an end game in mind. If you don't know where you want to go, you will never be able to plan how to get there."

One of the most important parts of my list of "P's" is PLANNING your PATH. Planning is very important in life because it provides you with a clear path toward the pursuit of your goals. People have confidence in people who plan. It lets them know that you aren't just guessing about how to accomplish your purpose. It says that you are serious about moving forward, and you aren't just winging it. People want to follow someone with a plan. If you want to make sure your obituary won't suck, it's important that you have a plan for your life in the four key areas discussed earlier in the book.

As I said previously, it doesn't matter where you are in life...poor, unemployed, in a job you hate, in a bad relationship, parenting a rebellious child, working for a horrible boss, or happy and just wanting to move to an even better place in life, you are only one decision and three action steps away from transforming your life from where you are, to where you want to be.

LET ME SAY THAT AGAIN...YOU ARE ONLY ONE DECISION AND THREE ACTION STEPS AWAY FROM TRANSFORMING YOUR LIFE FROM WHERE YOU ARE, TO WHERE YOU WANT TO BE.

If you are in circumstances that you do not like, or want to move to another level in life, all you need to do is the following:

• Write down where you want to be in three to five years from now.

• Write down three things that you need to do within the next 12 months to make that happen.

• Write down three things that you need to do within the next 90 days to make that happen.

Once you decide where you want to go, have written down the three action steps to take within a year, and the three action steps to take within the next 90 days, all you need to do is GO...TAKE ACTION. Once you decide to go, you take the first three action steps that you have written down in your plan. Every time you complete three action steps, write three more down. Success is always being able to do the next three action steps successfully. Before you know it, it's five years later, and you have accomplished your big goal just by acting on all the small steps that you needed to get there.

When you begin to think through your life plan, there are four areas that you need to have annual goals for, and put thought into:

Relationships

Relationships are everywhere in your life. It's what this entire book is about. People will build you up or tear you down. Have a plan to develop your relationships to help be a building process in your life.

Career - Business

The number one driver of your financial health is your career or business development. It is how you make money that funds the quality of life you want. With financial pressures being the number one stress on marriage, business, and life in general, it is very important to have annual goals and a plan to maintain growth in your professional career or business. Your goals don't have to be lofty goals…they just need to be aiming you towards growing towards the quality of life that you want.

Physical Health

I've learned in life, you should never make decisions when you are tired or not feeling well. A big part of being physically healthy is making sure that you get enough rest, eat right, and have a continuous, consistent routine of physical activity that provides the energy you need to be successful, day in and day out. I will address this more in depth in a later chapter.

Finances

I remember giving my son a birthday card that read,

"Money isn't everything, but it sure makes life easier." As I said earlier, financial pressures cause great stress in life, and is the number one reason that many marriages struggle today. Financial insecurity plays a huge role in the emotions of a family. When things are tight, attitudes are tight. It is important that you have a plan of financial growth to relieve those pressures. I'm going to talk about this as well, in a later chapter.

Life planning doesn't have to be complicated or long range. So many people spend so much time doing comprehensive five- and ten-year-plans, when the things that impact their plan are going to change dramatically in the next three years. With technology, the economy, and many other things changing at such a rapid pace, things change way too fast to think in terms of five- and ten-year-plans in my opinion. Think in short term increments to obtain a long-term dream or goal. I will talk later about how to put an effective life plan together, and how often to review it.

A plan allows you to work through each facet that can impact you and prepare you for it so that you stay on a clear path to your goals. Life comes at us fast, and it is easy to veer off course. The next thing you know, what was going to take you two years to accomplish, is now going to take you four years because you got off track and make a bad choice.

Imagine if you were in Miami, Florida and you were given the goal of being in Seattle, Washington in seven days. That is a 3,300-mile journey. At 500 miles a day, that would take you almost seven days. If you left Miami without a map in hand or GPS, you would never make it there in seven days. You wouldn't know what direction to go, and any obstacles that may come up to delay your trip. By planning and looking at the proper resources ahead of time, you are able to determine the quickest path to your destination, without the headache of being lost or delayed. You can pre-think any unforeseen obstacles that might delay your trip, like weather, traffic, and potential accidents, and even plan an alternate route to get around the delay, but a map or GPS is your best plan to help you get there on time.

Life and business are the same way. In order to accomplish your goals, it is important that you work through a plan that sets your path clearly in the direction of your goals. It is important that you sit down and think about your goals on a consistent basis and brainstorm the things that might delay your plans, so you can come up with solutions to the "what if this happens" scenarios. The key in the "what if this happens" review, is to focus on the things you can control. So many people get caught up in worrying over the things that they can't control, and they forget that they actually have numerous actions they can take to influence their path in life, and keep it moving forward.

I always say when things happen that disrupt people's lives, "People can't see the forest for the trees, and they forget to look down and see that there is a chainsaw right beside them to cut the trees down." Sometimes it pays to look around in the midst of adversity. The solutions to the obstacles blocking your path are typically right near you.

This doesn't mean that you ignore all of the things that you can't control. You do take the time to work through them and write down a contingency plan in the event that it actually happens, but you don't let it take your focus away from the action steps that you actually can take.

Another key part of planning is, "You need to quit planning for a future that you cannot predict and start creating the future you WANT!" It's a totally different mindset when you pursue what you want. Most people wander around, lost in disbelief, because they can't predict the future, and forget that they actually have control over many things that can help them to achieve their purpose and goals.

The key to any plan is to have it written down someplace. If it's written down, you remember it and can be held accountable for it. A plan without accountability is no plan at all. When you are writing your plan down, you want to make sure that you have a stated set of goals at the top. From there, you write down the action steps that you need to take in order to achieve your goals in the next 12 months and the next 90 days. Beside each action step, you should have what you need to accomplish, a date to accomplish it by, and any people listed who can help you succeed in that action step.

Your success in your life plan will depend on the Pillars and Characteristics that I outlined in my *Path to the Ultimate Life* visual. How you respond to challenges along the way will also determine your rate of success. Never see challenges as an end to your dreams and goals. Challenges are opportunities to learn and grow in perseverance. Never give up. Never quit. If things don't seem to be going right, you may need to make changes in your plan in order to achieve your goals.

As you are living out your life plan, it's important that you review it at periodic points so that you can make sure you are on the right course. I always suggest looking at a life plan every quarter. With things changing in the world so fast, you want to be able to adjust your plan as the environment around you changes. Your review should be as easy as asking the following questions:

- Where should I be in pursuing my goal?
- Where am I?
- What I am doing that I should be doing differently?
- What am I not doing that I should not be doing?
- What should I stop doing because it's done, or wast-

ing my time?

• A plan of attack to make up the difference, if there is a gap between where I should be, and where I actually am.

The problem with any planning in life is that many do not write them down...leaving themselves to wing it. A year later, they are wondering why they are still in the same place, spinning their wheels. The key in making a plan your reality, is to write it down, act on it, review it, adjust if needed, and repeat the process.

Your plan should be specific enough to keep you on course towards your purpose, but agile and flexible enough to take on new opportunities that may allow you to fulfill your purpose and reach your goal even quicker...in a way that you never even thought possible.

As you work on your life plan, there are two areas you will want to make sure that you think through:

Identify Your Threats to Achieving Your Purpose & Goals

On your journey towards achieving your purpose, various obstacles are going to get in your way. They may be the economy, an ineffective boss, divorce, or a competitor. Regardless of what they are, you need to identify what those threats are, and then determine whether they are controllable or uncontrollable. If they are uncontrollable, write down what you should do as a contingency, if it were to occur. If it is controllable, this is where you want to put your real effort. I have found in my life, that most people are so worried about what they can't control, that they forget to be 100% effective and focused on what they can control. Have the action steps that you may have to take for the uncontrollable things in your life, but 100% of your effort should be focused on all of the things that you DO HAVE CONTROL of on your path to success.

Identify the Resources and People That You Have at Your Disposal to Achieve Your Purpose and Goals

These are the tools and network that you will use to overcome the obstacles in step one and take advantage of the opportunities that come your way. Resources may be your job, your network of people, or training that you are involved in. After you have a full list of resources, brainstorm what resources you still need to acquire to be more effective in achieving your purpose and goals for life. Once you have this full list, you have all the tools that you need to be successful.

I want to end this chapter on the area of finances, because it is a biggie. It is so important for you to have a financial plan in the areas of meeting monthly expenses, liquidity for unforeseen expenses, and retirement planning.

Ever since I was 20 years old, I have had an Excel spreadsheet budget. It has helped me to look at the reality of what I can and cannot afford. So many live above their means because they don't know that they don't have enough money to pay their bills. They keep rolling up debt with credit cards and credit lines, to live a lifestyle that they can't afford. Planning your monthly financial budget is easy. Whether you write them down or use an Excel spreadsheet, do the following:
- Make twelve columns, one for each month
- Put a total column at the end for the year
- Write all sources of income on the first line for each month

- Write your monthly expenses in for each month
- Add each column up at the bottom

You will quickly see what months you have extra income or a deficit, and how much money you should have at the end of the year. This is usually an eye-opener for most people because it shows them how much money they have to spend after bills. This is the number one reason that people don't do budgeting, because they don't want to see the reality of what they can't spend money on. Instead, they just keep spending and racking up debt. They want to keep "robbing Peter to pay Paul." Don't let yourself get in this rut. Do an annual budget to see where you lack and start planning on how you can enhance your income to achieve your financial goals. Remember, in my opinion, financial pressures are the number one reason for stress in many marriages, businesses, and just life in general. Make a yearly financial budget so you can plan to minimize those pressures.

When it comes to "financial liquidity" for the unexpected, it is crucial that you have one of two items: 1) money in savings, or 2) a credit card that you can access to pay for a big expenditure. This must be with the intent that you will pay it off in a short period of time…like three to four months. Always have a way to pay for $500 to $2,000 for an unexpected event…they are going to happen…that's life. Just when you don't need it to happen, your car will break down, your home air conditioner will give out, or a big medical bill will occur. Budget this in every year so you can have peace of mind that you are always prepared for it.

When it comes to retirement, many people think the illustrious notion of retirement, "just happens." They spend their entire life having fun, and then wake up at sixty with the reality that they don't have enough saved to quit working. What you need to know though, is that one of the greatest things ever created for us was compound interest. Compound interest is interest that continues to accumulate on top of itself, over time, with your investments. Over a span of twenty years, it will amount to more money than you would have thought when you first started investing on day one.

I wasn't taught this at a young age and didn't start thinking about retirement savings until I was 48. The amount that I am having to put away, to one day fully retire and enjoy life, is seven times the amount of money that my children would have to put away, if they start at age 25. If you don't start early, the amount of money you have to put away each month can almost be too much.

I can remember when the IRA deduction was $1,000 a year while in my 20s. I can remember saying to myself, that won't amount to anything over time. When you do the math, it really does add up. While writing this book, I did a little study of my life earnings. I wondered what would have been the impact of my life savings had I learned to live without just five percent of my annual wages and invested the five percent in a set of highly rated mutual funds that follow the S & P 500. Most experts will tell you that over the long term, you will get somewhere around twelve percent a year on average, investing over twenty plus years. I discounted the rate of return to ten percent, just to be conservative. Knowing this, I did a spreadsheet, taking 10% of my earnings since age twenty-two and adding interest to that annual savings each year to see what my life savings for retirement would be at 65. I was surprised that my pot of money to retire with would have been over $1,200,000! Yes, I said one point two million dollars.

Failing to do this type of planning will leave you somewhat desperate near retirement because you will be left with whatever social security is going to pay when you reach retirement age. Don't get caught at any age thinking that retirement just happens, or social security will be enough. It doesn't just happen, and social security will not be enough. Plan, and plan early, even if it is just putting away $100 a month into an IRA. To see the reality of this visually, I want you to take a close look at the following visual that I created when I was in financial planning. It represents the four stages of life:

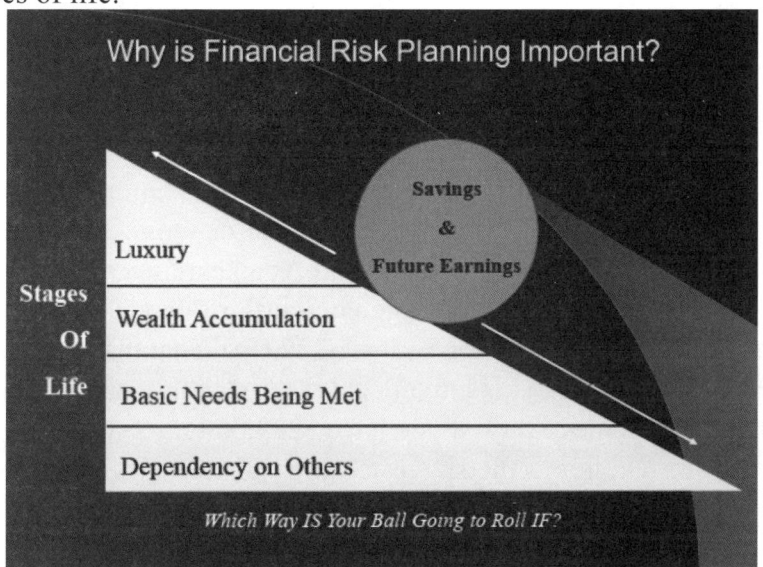

Stage one is childhood through college. From birth to college, almost everyone is dependent on parents, grandparents, family, and friends.

Stage two is mid 20s and early marriage. During our 20s and early 30s, many get married, have children, and pretty much are meeting their basic needs. It can be tough to save much on your own given the expense of a home and children. This is a good stage in which to try and land a job with a good company that offers some type of matched retirement plan.

Stage three is your mid 30s through retirement. 35 to 60 is traditionally a person's highest, and prime earning years, and is where wealth accumulation happens. Expenses should begin to lower in your late 50s with children graduating college and no longer dependent on you for financial needs.

Stage four is supposed to be actual retirement. You spend your entire life pushing the ball of savings up the hill, hoping to get to the final stage and retire.

The real data from a study done in 2000, by the Social Security Office of Research and Statistics, tells us that of all adults who reach 25 years of age, 16% will pass on before age 65, 18% will be financially independent, and 66% will have their "ball" roll all the way back down the hill at age 65, and be dependent on others for one or more: housing, healthcare, transportation, and food. You heard me....66%!

If you look at the average net worth of people age 65, as reported by CNN Money, it is $232,000. That may sound like a lot of money to some people...especially young people. Here is the reality: if you have $232,000 in savings, and you are taking out the suggested four percent a year by financial planning experts, so you don't run out of money too quickly, you will be living on an annual income of $9,280. If you add another estimated $18,000 from Social Security, that's only $27,280 a year. You can't pay for housing, transportation, healthcare, and food required at retirement on $2,273 a month. It's no wonder 66% of people reaching age 65 are reliant on others to live out the rest of their life.

If you are one of those 66%, that means you're relying on your kids, family, and maybe friends for healthcare, living expenses, housing, etcetera. If they aren't there for you, who will take care of you and where will you live? Nursing homes are filled with parents whose children never come see them. Will this be you?

I want to highly, highly encourage everyone reading this book to take the time to sit down NOW and access your financial risk plan. Things that cause the ball to roll backwards include divorce, daughter's wedding (or weddings if you have more than one daughter), paying for college for your children, unexpected disability/death, taxes, job change, being fired/down-sized, etc. These are all "threats" to your idea of retirement in the future, and a good quality of life. The earlier you put a plan in place, the less expensive it is to cover the risk and do something about it. If you want to have a $60,000 a year income at 65, if Social Security pays you $20,000 a year, you need at least $1,000,000 in the bank, just to take out the four percent suggested by financial planning experts. Are you on target to have a million in savings at age 65? If not, it's time to get serious about your plan...NOW. The biggest threat to your plan is choosing NOT TO PLAN.

As you are looking at the four areas I have shared, take a look at your professional career or business, and ask yourself, "Is it helping build my four key areas of life, or is it taking away from my four key areas discussed at the beginning of this chapter?" If it's not building, and you are not happy, you may want to look at making a change. Don't let your career drive who you are, or how you live your life. Let your life, and who you are, drive your career. Your heart and soul will love you for it and your obituary won't suck for sure.

Before you leave this chapter, stare at the four stages of life graph that I shared earlier:

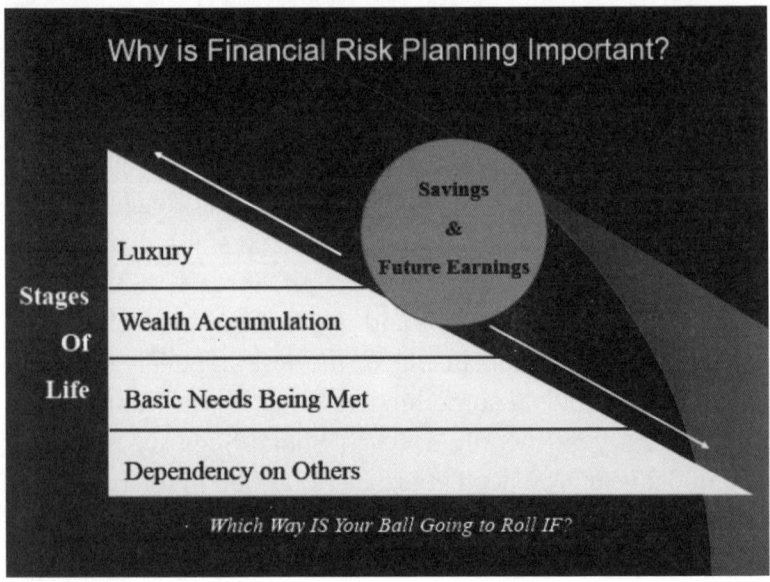

Where are you on the graph? Is the reality that you will be relying on others after age 65? Don't let another day go by without putting some thought into where you are, where you want to be, and a plan to make up the gap if one exists. Look at each area of relationships, spiritual, physical, and financial. When you are in the second half of your life, you will be very happy you did.

APPLICATION TO MAXIMIZE YOUR DASH

What do you need to improve in your relationships to reach the quality of life you want?

What areas of your spiritual life do you need to be better at? Does your spiritual belief align with your behaviors?

What do you need to do differently in your physical life to be able to stay healthy for your family, employees, and friends?

On a scale from 1 to 10, with 10 being on target, and 1 not being on target, rate yourself on:

- Meeting your monthly expenses without credit card debt
- Having the means to pay for an unexpected bill
- Being on target at your current age to retire at age 65

What do you have to do in order to be better at managing your finances?

What are you willing to sacrifice to help you save the money for your future?

ACTION STEPS TO MAXIMIZE YOUR DASH

Where do you want to be in three years in the following areas:

Relationships:

Spiritually:

Physically:

Financially:

Write down your three action steps that you need to make in the next 90 days and in 12 months, in the following areas, to put you on track to reach your goals:

90 Day Action Steps

1)

2)

3)

12 Month Action Steps

1)

2)

3)

CHAPTER 15

PAUSE AND MEDITATION

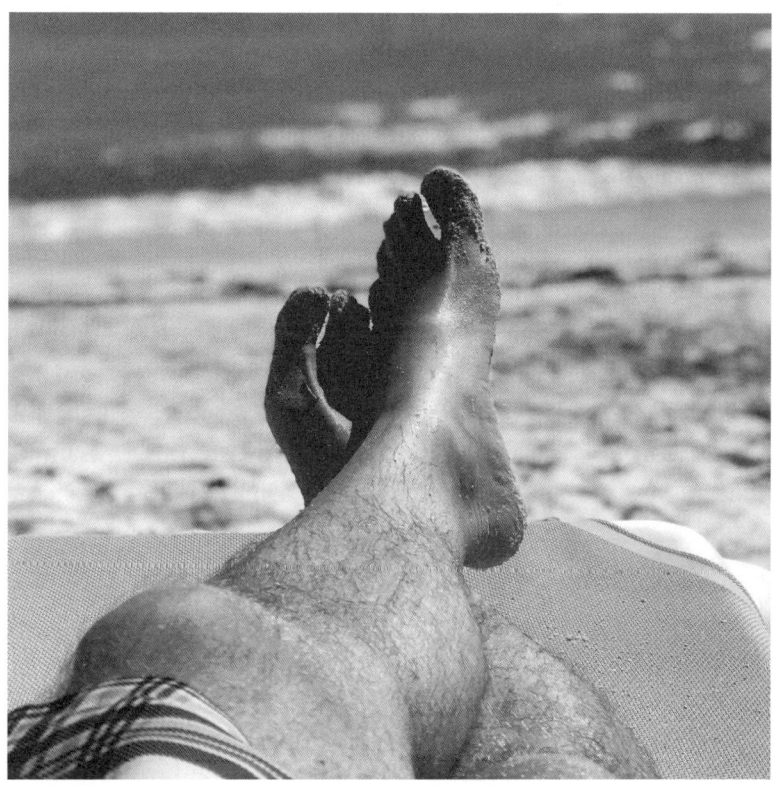

"It's in the moment of pause that you confirm you are headed the right direction, or that you need to shift to another direction."

So, let's look at where you are at this point in the book. You have worked on defining your PURPOSE, discovering your PASSION, deciding on PRINCIPLES, setting your PRIORITIES, looking at the PEOPLE you need to surround yourself with, and working through your PAST. Now you have a solid PLAN to obtain the life you want. You are ready to go! But wait...there is a moment when we have to pause and think about our plan and path.

Pausing for a moment is so crucial, because some of us can be selfish in what we are wanting in life. Some people are impulsive in how they pursue life, and some people have made a series of bad choices in the past. It is a healthy thing, after all of these steps, to pause and just let all of your plans settle a bit.

People love to be associated with people who take time to pause and meditate on things that are meaningful. It gives them confidence that you won't be running into something without thinking about it. Do people like people who are pioneers? Of course they do. I'm a huge pioneer in life, but I have learned when to be a pioneer, and when to pause and meditate before acting. The bigger the risk, the more reason to pause and meditate. If you want to make sure your obituary won't suck, it is important that you pause and meditate on your plans and even take the time to share your plan with someone that you trust to look at it, and give you sound feedback.

Anytime you work through your life plan, at any level, it is going to create change. It is a good step to take a few days and sit on the ideas, discuss them with your closest friends/mentors, and make sure that you have thought of everything. Now, not every decision needs this kind of pause, but many should, especially if you feel that your past decisions have caused you to veer off course in your life. You need someone who has a history of making good decisions that created success, to help you talk through what you are about to do.

My life has benefited tremendously through the close friendships that I have had throughout my life. They are people who know my heart, know how I think, and know my dreams and desires. At any given time, I could get on the phone or meet them in person and discuss any major decision in my life or business and receive invaluable feedback.

I've already told the story of the friend who encouraged me to start my singles ministry. He knew my heart and passion to make a difference in single adults who were struggling in the world of relationships. I was getting ready to gear up a plan to look at other jobs, when in my moment of pause, he encouraged me to think about another route. Out of that pause came an organization, that over three years, reached over 10,000 single adults, from over 150 churches. Many shared their stories about how JaxMetroLive played a major role in them finding their purpose in life, walking away from drugs…the bar scene, and in getting their life on the right track. I'm so glad I chose to pause and talk about my plan with my friend.

I can remember another time, well into my singles ministry, when it wasn't bringing in enough money to fully support me as a full-time staff person. I was holding out for it to happen and allowing my family to suffer financially. I got caught up in the moment, with wanting to do my passion full-time. It wasn't happening fast enough, but because I was so emotionally invested, I kept pounding the pavement for the funding to create the success that it needed in order to support me as a full-time staff position. I didn't realize at first the impact that it was having on my marriage and our family unit. But overtime it became very clear.

So, I came up with this new plan for funding for the ministry and called one of my closest friends to talk about it. He was very successful, well thought out, and knew me long before the ministry took off. The call to him was my way of pausing to see if I had the right things in order. The conversation didn't go the way I wanted it to. He proceeded to have a hard conversation with me. He knew my wife and I as a couple and could see the difficulty that my staying in the ministry was putting on our family. He proceeded to have a hard conversation with me saying, "Tom, your family needs you to use your talents in other ways to make sure the mortgage is paid, and they have food on the table. You need to go out this week and find a job, so you can work while the ministry gains enough funding to make it full-time." He went on to discuss with me that my wife would see that as a positive action on my part…that I was willing to do "whatever it takes" to make sure my family had a home, food, and that we could cover our bills. I was like…WOAH! This is not the conversation that I was looking to have. The ministry had been changing hundreds of people's lives every week, and I didn't want to leave that full-time. I wanted to stay in it, and I had a plan to make it happen. But in my moment of "pause and meditation", my friend spoke the truth into my life that I needed to hear.

I was ready to dive in and work to create more funding, when what I really needed to do was to go get a job. Within the next week, I met with the coach of my kids' flag football team. He was one of the partners in a nationally growing sub shop. I discussed with him the management opportunities within their company. He saw that I had the type of qualities that they were looking for in their store management teams and hired me within the week. Over the course of the next year, I saw a change in my relationship with my wife, in that she saw a husband who was willing to do whatever it took to make sure that our family had enough money to make our bills and take the financial pressure off.

This wouldn't have happened had I not taken the time to pause and meditate on my plan and discuss it with someone close to me. Had I gone ahead with my plan, I would have created more pressure in my family than was already there.

Remember, pausing and meditating on your plan, isn't only to confirm that you have everything needed for your plan to be successful. Pausing and meditating on your plan is also to determine if you should even follow through with your plan.

Sometimes in your moment of pause and meditation, when you seek outside counsel from people, you may not hear what you want to hear. Be cautious to NOT turn away their comments, simply because they didn't tell you what you wanted to hear. Be open and listen to what they are saying, because you are so emotionally invested in your decision, that you may not be seeing things clearly. I'm a big believer that if you ask three of your mentors/friends about your plan, and you explain fully to them your plan, and they all tell you it's not a good course of action, then it's probably a plan that you need to seriously rethink.

The big key for pausing and meditating on your life or business plans, is to surround yourself with a network of at least three to four mentors, who are willing to listen to you and have honest conversations about your plan. Remember what I talked about in the chapter on people? You want to make sure the people you are surrounding yourself with are the ones headed in the same successful direction as you are.

APPLICATION TO MAXIMIZING YOUR DASH

What is your biggest challenge with pausing and meditating on big decisions in your life?

What is your biggest challenge, talking about your plans or decisions, with key mentors or friends before you act?

How does it make you feel when you hear someone say, "I don't think that making that decision is in your best interest?"

When you look at the key decisions in your life that you rushed into, how did those decisions turn out? Were there friends telling you not to make that choice? Why didn't you listen?

ACTION STEPS TO MAXIMIZING YOUR DASH

What decisions do you have coming up that you feel you need to pause and meditate on?

Who are three people that you can call for personal and/or business feedback for decisions that you want another opinion on?

CHAPTER 16

LET'S GET PHYSICAL

"The decisions that you make in the first half of your life regarding your health, will determine how you get to live out the second half of your life... Take it seriously."

I know what you are thinking...OMG, Tom is about to tell me I'm out of shape and I need to workout, diet, and step on the scale every Friday morning. Well, I'm not going to do that...well, maybe just a little. Why? Because your physical health is the fuel that gives you the daily energy to make sure your obituary won't suck.

Listen up. I'm here to tell you from personal experience, that you need to take a serious look in the mirror, and ask yourself, "What are you doing to keep yourself healthy, and in good physical shape?" It doesn't matter what age you are, you still need to have a weekly plan for physical activity. It needs to include some level of cardio (to keep your heart healthy and strong), and strength training (to keep your body healthy and strong), and it doesn't have to be one and two hours in the gym. It can be swimming, biking, running, as well as, high intensity strength training sets in your own living room...and it only has to last for 30 minutes at a time. Everyone's got 30 minutes of time for their health.

If you want the number on the right side of the Dash to stay blank for many years, then you need to have a plan for your health. You want to be able to have the energy to put forth the effort to help a friend move, work a few hours extra on an important project, or just do something athletic with your friends, kids, or grandkids. That comes with good health at any age.

If you are young, let me help you to understand the "why" in all of this physical health stuff. If you are under 30 and you are over your height versus weight limit, have any type of adverse health conditions, then you need to think seriously about having a weekly plan that includes a healthy diet, and at least 30 minutes of working out, at least five times a week. As I said above, all it takes is 30 minutes a day. If you don't take your health (and weight) seriously, then once you hit your forties and fifties, you will pay the price.

If you are young and slim, let me wake you up a bit. I have been an athlete my entire life. I played baseball in middle school, high school, and college. I ran cross-country in college. I ran in my 20s and have pretty much worked out off-and-on for my entire life. I also engaged in intramural sports like golf, ultimate Frisbee, and basketball in my 30s and 40s. I haven't played as much in my 40s and 50s as I once did, but I have always worked out. When I graduated high school, I weighed 135 pounds and had a 29" waist. I was slim, strong, and could run like a deer…forever. When I hit my late 20s, I was 160 pounds and had a 32" waist. I thickened up and filled out, and it actually looked good on me. I was growing into manhood, but by the time I hit my late 30s, I hit 190 pounds and had a 34" waist. BOOM! When I hit 45, I had a 38" waist at 210 pounds…AND I AM A HIGHLY ACTIVE GUY!

Since 45, I have eaten healthy and consistently worked out…just to maintain my waistline, weight, and health. I tell you this as young people to let you know, if you let your body go, it's going to really go in your late 30s and 40s, and will be hard to get back in your 50s…especially, if you have fun habits like eating the wrong (albeit delicious) foods, and drinking socially. Build good habits while you are young. That doesn't mean you can't have fun but enjoy everything in moderation. Build good habits into your life with a consistent workout and healthy eating. Your body will love you for it, you will feel better every day, and you will give yourself a chance to live a longer life and enjoy each day physically.

Now, let me talk to the people over 30. It's not too late to make a choice to take your health back. The combination of what you put into your body, and the lack of physical activity in your life, is doing more harm than you can even imagine. At the end of this chapter, I'm going to give you some "do's" and "don'ts" for your life, to help you be committed to being physically healthy.

As I reached my 50s, I happened to attend a conference

in Atlanta, Georgia. Many people reading this book have been to professional conferences and know what I'm talking about with regards to all-you-can-eat events during the day, and hospitality at night. After returning from the conference in Atlanta, I did a lot of self-analyzing about what I experienced with regards to calorie consumption for the days that I was at the conference. Atlanta and its sponsors rolled out the red carpet for the attendees, as any city does for a big conference, and attendees greatly appreciated it…especially me. I love to eat and love a social drink (or two). As I looked at what we were all putting into our bodies over the four-day period, I began to really take a hard look at what many people put into their bodies on a daily basis. Being married to a Personal Fitness Trainer put it right in my face. We began to discuss the fact that reports show that two-thirds of the American adult population are overweight and have very poor eating and workout habits. My questions for you at this point are:

- Do you want to be physically prepared to make the best decisions in your life and business?
- Do you want to be physically able to enjoy the fun outdoor activities that life offers?
- Do you want to be around when your grandkids are born?
- Do you want to see your grandkids grow up, and enjoy playing with them?
- Do you want to enjoy the last ten years of your life without physical ailments?

If the answers to these questions are YES, then you need to pay attention to this chapter and build the good habits that will allow you to live out those four questions above. Studies show that upwards of 80% of healthcare costs come from behavior and lifestyle choices that people make. These choices include, but are not limited to: poor diet, lack of exercise, smoking, lack of sleep, and/or excessive drinking. These behaviors can lead to obesity, high blood pressure, diabetes, stroke, heart attack, and metabolic syndrome, just to name a few. Now, I'm not trying to throw fear around lightly, but rather, trying to be real about the consequences of your daily habits and choices, with regards to the serious over consumption of calories, and lack of physical activity in today's lifestyle. We love to drink it up. We love our fast food. We love our greasy, fried foods...our highly-processed foods... our sugary yummies, and we love our soft drinks. We love. We love. We love!!! You should love to live a LONG LIFE.

Now let me dial it back here for a second. I'm not advocating that you give up everything I just talked about; there is absolutely nothing wrong with having a happy hour. There is nothing wrong with eating fried foods. There is nothing wrong with having fast food. There is nothing wrong with enjoying a sweet treat. BUT, it should all be in moderation. Before I met my wife, I was eating fast food at least three times; sometimes four times a week. That probably wasn't good for my health. Fast food is very tasty, but not overly nutritious, and should be done in moderation.

I personally live a very active and fun life in my 50s. I love networking, being out at social events, and doing physically challenging things in work and life, especially with my wife and kids. Life is meant to be lived, right? Well I do! I come at life with a lot of energy, do a lot of crazy stuff that many say they can't do, and typically will dance until late into the night with my wife and friends.

Many ask, "Tom, how do you do it?" Well, in my early 30s, I didn't need to have a plan because the calories just fell off my body, and weight just stayed away. In my late 40s, those same calories began to hang on for dear life, and the weight was like a magnet to my body. I knew that if I kept eating like crazy, with no plan for a healthy lifestyle in my 40s and 50s, I was sure to drive my health into the ground. Deteriorating health plays a huge role in your ability to enjoy your life as you grow older. Your decisions that you make for your body before thirty years of age will have a big impact on how your physical health will be in your forties and fifties.

When my kids and friends are wanting to go out dancing, kayaking, mountain biking, zip-lining, skiing, white water rafting or playing some basketball, I didn't want my body to say "no." I came to the conclusion that I needed to think and act differently with each decade, to ensure I am able to keep enjoying the things I love, well into retirement. It all starts with habits in your 20s and 30s, and redefining discipline in your 40s and 50s.

With the help of my wife, a Personal Trainer and Health and Wellness Coach, I've developed a balance of disciplined eating, moderation, and fitness, that keeps my body feeling young, energetic, and fit. Three things I've learned about keeping your body at a weight that you feel good at and staying healthy are:

- 80% of weight/fat loss (or weight/fat gain) comes from the kitchen (what you eat).
- You can NEVER workout more than the calories you consume…there's just not enough hours in a day.
- To get the weight off, and have the toned body you desire, you MUST do both: disciplined eating AND fitness.

For those of you who say, "Tom, I travel too much, or don't have the time", your excuses can disappear. There are workouts now that you can do right in your living room or hotel room from an app on your mobile device such as Beach

Body On Demand. All you need is your own body weight and a couple of dumbbells. If you travel, you can structure a highly effective workout to do in your hotel room. If you are busy, you can take 30 minutes of your time, instead of watching a nightly television show. The question is, do you want it bad enough? Are you tired of feeling tired? Are you tired of not fitting into the clothes you would love to wear? Are you tired of not being able to do the things that you want to do, because you are not physically able to do them?

I'm encouraging you, whether you are 20 years old, over 50, or in between, get serious about your health. It's a small investment each day, and the benefits are huge. You will feel better, move better, and look better. You will be more confident in life and work. Your relationships will flourish, because your spouse or significant other will see how important you feel it is to be in good health for them.

To help you walk away with some applicable take-aways in this chapter that will transform your life, I've put together a list of "10 do's" and "10 don'ts" to help you be more pro-active in managing your health. These 20 small action steps will help you work towards a healthier, and long-lasting life, so your obituary won't suck. These tips come from my wife, DeAnna, a Certified Personal Trainer and Corporate Health and Wellness Coach:

10 Things You SHOULD Do Weekly

- Eat...don't skip meals BUT choose wisely (think veggies and lean proteins at every meal).
- Pack your own healthy snacks to carry in your bag. This will help you to avoid making bad choices because of low blood sugar.
- Choose veggies and fruit over other less healthy

choices like bread, pasta, and dessert.
- Eat dessert, BUT only have a bite or two.
- Drink like a fish…WATER.
- When drinking mixed drinks, let the mixer be water.
- Take your vitamins because most of us don't eat enough healthy, whole foods to meet the RDA on many important vitamins and minerals.
- Try to get eight hours of sleep.
- Make time to sweat…every day (even 15-20 minutes of exercise is better than nothing).
- Have a glass of water in between each "adult" beverage.

10 Things You Should NOT Be Doing Weekly

- You should NOT be consuming high calorie/high carb breakfast goodies (bagels, doughnuts, pastries).
- You should NOT be eating the bread and butter on the table.
- You should NOT be indulging in the high calorie/ high fat snacks.
- You should NOT be drinking soda…not even diet.
- You should NOT be eating the temptations at the office (candy, cookies, cakes, and other junk food).
- You should NOT do "seconds" …only one pass through the buffet.
- You should NOT be grazing from the floating appetizer trays at parties and events (or at most, only have one).
- You should NOT partake in the sweet, fancy, "fluffy" mixed drinks (there can be as many as several hundred calories in EACH drink, wine has the fewest calories).

- You should NOT sit for long periods of time (you burn more calories standing and walking).
- You should NOT go out with the attitude that you'll eat, drink, and be merry with reckless abandon…it WILL be waiting for you when you get home and step on the scale.

…and remember, along with these 20 shifts in thinking, find a good mobile workout program that you can do anytime, anywhere. Technology is making health and fitness a piece of cake. WAIT, DID I JUST SAY A PIECE OF CAKE? NOT IN THIS CHAPTER!

With a disciplined diet, moderation, and a sound fitness program, you can maintain a healthy lifestyle that will keep your waistline slim, healthcare costs down, and maximize the enjoyment of a long life.

Make a personal commitment to change your habits for your spouse, kids, family, friends, and co-workers who depend on you. Years down the road, you will say it was the best decision that you ever made, and you'll be adding years to your life, and life to your years.

APPLICATION TO MAXIMIZING YOUR DASH

What don't you like about yourself physically?

What are your challenges with eating a healthy diet on a regular basis?

Why don't you work out? If you do, how can you ensure that you stay disciplined?

What could you change about your schedule that would make time for 30 minutes each day to do some cardio and strength training?

Write down the people in your life who are worth your effort to start a strategy for healthy living.

ACTION STEPS TO MAXIMIZING YOUR DASH

What is your physical goal in the next 12 months to get yourself in better shape?

How are you going to change your eating habits in the next week to build good habits with your diet?

CHAPTER 17

PREPARATION AND PRACTICE

"In life, preparation without practice will minimize creativity, and leave you open to unforeseen circumstances to get in the way of your quality of life. Practice creates innovation and flushes out the obstacles so you can prepare how to sidestep them if they occur."

If there is one area of life that is definitely like sports, it's PRACTICE AND PREPARATION. Excellence comes from creating good habits in practice, and preparation. Just as a football coach, or player, looks at a playbook and studies film before any game, it is important for you, in your life and business decisions, to study your life playbook that you are forming as you read this book.

I highly recommend that you write your decisions down for each of the areas that I have been talking about in this book. Put them into a "Life Action Plan" journal. I have talked extensively about why you need to have a plan for your life. I want to reinforce the importance of writing your plan down. This will provide a road map for you to stay on course and live your life, while remaining flexible for opportunity and unexpected fun experiences. At the end of the book, there is a list of the key areas that you need to make choices for in your Life Action Plan.

My wife and I put our annual budget and life goals for our four key areas in an Excel spreadsheet. Once a quarter we have a life planning date night and we review and practice our plan to ensure that our goals are moving us toward the life we continually want. We do it quarterly because life around us changes so fast. Opportunities and challenges develop quickly, and we want to be able to adjust our plan in real time to keep it dynamic and meeting our goals.

Once you have your Life Action Plan in writing, you then can practice and prepare throughout your life for the path you will take in the pursuit of your ultimate life. Having a Life Action Plan gives you a visual document that you can sit down with on a quarterly basis and think about where you are and where you are headed in life. As you look at where you are headed, you can pre-think where you want to be in the future and look at where you are supposed to be and make changes in your plan if there is a gap. Preparation without practice in life and business limits your creative ideas and leaves you unprepared for unexpected circumstances that can have a negative impact on your life. Had you "practiced" what you "prepared" for, you would have, at some point said, "What if we were able to (insert idea)." …Or you may say, "You know, as I think through this, my concern is (insert concern)." If all you do is prepare, you will get caught up in the details that can deter you from seeing new ideas and threats to your success.

I recommend this process for any aspect of your life, including: preparing for what college you will attend, what major you pick, the interview process when looking for a job, having kids, choosing a career, opening your own company, and all major decisions within that company. Preparing and practicing will maximize your success the most cost effectively and efficiently.

Let me share with you how preparation and practice have made a huge difference in my life, both personally and professionally.

In 1996, I directed and planned my first big trade show and conference for my first association. It went quite well. We had great attendance compared to their past shows, and reviews were very positive. I worked from my company's timeline of "Things To Do" to plan the event that was there before I was hired. I had never planned an event of this magnitude, so I thought this was the way it was done. The show went great, but I believed it could have been much better. I was determined to make 1997 an amazing expo and conference. Our team went into the planning process, as we did in 1996, but we bit off more than we could chew. We expanded the expo, increased the amount of educational sessions, and we had a location that put the expo and conference in two different buildings, a few blocks from each other. We had all the pieces to be successful, and we pursued it with the same planning process that we used before. As the show took place, there were a number of hiccups throughout the event that were brought out in our post show critique. I can remember the post show critique very vividly with my Board of Directors. There were small details here and there, that were missed because we bit off a larger plan than we could pull off with the number of staff that we had. We prepared big but didn't practice. Had we practiced the event in our minds, over and over in the planning process, we would have seen very clearly that we did not have the staff to do what we were planning for.

I made a commitment that year that I would never pursue anything that has a large and lasting impact without "practicing" the plan ahead of time as a part of the process. What I developed as a result, was an event-planning document that became our organization's "Playbook." After planning, practicing, and putting the Playbook together once for the meeting, we would meet every month, and sometimes twice a month, going through the playbook event by event. We played out the event in our minds, as if we were actually there. This allowed us to virtually live out and "practice" the event over and over again. Once on site, we would do one last walk through of the Playbook to ensure no final questions. Having worked through the Playbook twenty plus times before the event ensured that we had thought of every detail related to attendee experience and operational issues. This new process fostered the "What if we could do this?", and "What if this happens?" discussion. I've used this process for every event that I've planned both professionally and personally, and every single one of them have been executed with precision and excellence.

If you are a college student or unemployed looking for a job, how much are you preparing and practicing for the interview process? Your competition is tough in the job market. You must bring your "A game" to the interview, or you will get looked over. It is imperative that you look at how you dress for the interview; do you know the top fifty interview questions, and what you would answer? Do you know their company and industry, and do you have a set of five questions for them so they get a true sense that you are very interested in working for them? Employers want to know that you are just not looking for a job, but that you have a desire to make a difference in their company. Interviewing at that level takes preparation and practice. Consider having a friend sit on the company's website and ask you questions about them, to help you practice answering questions about the company. Have them ask you questions about yourself from the top fifty interview questions.

As I'm writing this book, my wife and I are already practicing retirement. We are a number of years away from retirement, but when we get there, we want to make sure that we are prepared, and have practiced it so that we have thought through all the things that could have a negative impact on our retirement experience. We have worked through living in a condo, a home, or traveling in an RV. When we travel, do we want to be in an RV, a pop-up camper with an SUV, or stay in hotels or Airbnb's? Do we really want a second condo to have a place to stay on vacations and rent out for another retirement revenue stream? Looking at what our monthly expenses will be, how many buckets of retirement income will we need?

As we research and mentally "practice" retirement, it is helping us to "prepare" effectively for retirement. It's those unexpected circumstances that you didn't plan for in life and retirement, that cause you to have to work longer or compromise your experience, because you deflated your retirement income.

The same holds true for every aspect of your life and business. For any major decisions, in your life or business, after you plan and prepare…PRACTICE, PRACTICE, PRACTICE. Through the "mental practice" you will discover new ways to approach your decision, discover what obstacles will get in your way, and become excellent at the execution phase of the decision.

On the following page I've referred to my **Path to the Ultimate Life** diagram as your centerpiece to prepare, practice, and execute on any life decision, along with the steps to take.

Steps to Effective Preparation and Practice

- What is the objective that you want to accomplish?
- What are the choices that you need to make to accomplish your objectives?
- How much money will you need to invest in order to accomplish your objectives?
- What is your time investment in order to accomplish your objectives?
- What people do I need to be networked with, or have access to, in order to accomplish my objectives?
- Do I have the right attitude to be successful pursuing my goals?
- What changes will I need to make in order to be successful?
- Am I willing to persevere and commit to the timeline and do whatever it takes?
- How and what, do I have to communicate in order to

be successful?

• Knowing the first nine answers, do I have what it takes?

Use these ten questions for any major decisions. If the answer to number ten is YES, then execute and pursue it with passion. Life demands that you bring your "A game." If you bring it every day, you will experience a life with more confidence, excitement, energy, and a winning attitude, and there's almost no possible way your obituary will suck!

APPLICATION TO MAXIMIZING YOUR DASH

Do you feel you adequately prepare and practice for big life decisions?

How often do you actually spend mentally practicing your life choices to ensure excellence in execution?

How can you improve your time spent in practicing life?

ACTION STEPS TO MAXIMIZING YOUR DASH

Take your next two big life decisions and work through the ten questions on "Steps to Effective Preparation and Practice."

Mentally think through, and play out, your next big life decision by writing down all of the ideas that you need in order to be successful…and obstacles that will prevent your success. Practice until there are no obstacles.

CHAPTER 18

THE PURSUIT

"If you don't like your circumstances in life, you are always one decision and three action steps from changing your life. The first step you must take is to PURSUE change."

Ahhh…the call to action to PURSUE. It is the thing that stops many people from being successful. It's easy to think about your purpose, find your passion and talk it over with people, but once you have done all of the planning, preparing, and practicing, you still need to take action. You still need to PURSUE! You need to JUMP! You need to GO! You need to PUT ACTION TO YOUR WORDS to achieve your ultimate life!

So many things hold people back at this point. Even people who have a solid chance of success, sit on their hands because of the fear of failure, experiences of their past, and even fear of the possibility of success.

If you are in high school and have a college that you want to go to but think that you can't afford it…try thinking again. Look at the *Path to the Ultimate Life* visual again. If you manage your time, money, people, and choices well, with perseverance, the ability to adapt, have good communication skills, and have an awesome attitude, then you can go to any college that you want to go to. Now you need to know that there are always limited slots open for any opportunity. If there are more applicants than slots, just know that not making it in is more about not having enough slots than about your work and qualifications. You may just need to keep trying, until the time is right, and the opportunity presents itself, but whatever you do…DON'T GIVE UP!!!

If you are a job seeker, and there is a position that you want at a certain level, then you need to make the CHOICE to do what it takes to have the necessary qualifications for that position. Network with the PEOPLE in the industry. Have the MONEY to make your bills until an opening becomes available. Invest the TIME in studying that company's business model to wow them in your interview. Get the necessary education/certification needed so you meet the requirements of the job you want. You may just need to keep trying, until the time is right, and the opportunity presents itself, but whatever you do…DON'T GIVE UP!!!

If you are a business executive and there is a market

or opportunity you want to pursue, the same applies. You must make a smart CHOICE on which market to pursue. You must be willing to invest the MONEY to market your company or yourself. Spend the TIME researching the market, and all the angles, to maximize your profits. Assemble the PEOPLE that you need in sales, marketing, operations, and production, to be successful. You may just need to keep trying, until the time is right, and the opportunity presents itself, but whatever you do…DON'T GIVE UP!!!

If you are someone who just wants to make a change in your life, then you must be willing to make the CHOICE to do what it takes…invest the TIME necessary, spend or save the MONEY needed, and reach out to the PEOPLE who can help you to make your change. …AND…You may just need to keep trying, until the time is right, and the opportunity presents itself, but whatever you do…DON'T GIVE UP!!!

Change could be moving from renting an apartment to owning a home. Change could be getting out of a toxic relationship. Change could be getting out of debt. Change could be losing weight to better your health. Change could be quitting smoking, drugs, or alcohol abuse. Change could be putting your family as your top priority, and not working seventy hours a week. Change could be pursuing your education.

Whatever the change, you need to take the step to PURSUE. Take the leap of faith once you have walked through the process that I talked about in the Plan, Preparation, and Practice chapters. Let me forewarn you, once you PURSUE, there WILL be speed bumps. Things that come along that will make you feel discouraged, and even want to give up. They may cause you to ask yourself, "Did I make the right choice?"

That is where the four characteristics discussed earlier

come into play. No matter whether you are a student wanting to go to a good college, a person seeking a great job, an executive looking to pursue a new market opportunity, or an at home mom wanting to make change, you will not succeed if you don't have the perseverance to not give up on your goal, the ability to adapt to the environmental changes that come your way, surround yourself with the people you need to succeed, and communicate your goal well to those in your path.

The ability to pursue with confidence isn't about being 100% sure of success. No one can ever be 100% sure of success. Heck, 50% of businesses started, fail within the first five years. Fifty percent of first marriages end in divorce, and 41% of freshmen never graduate college.

In my opinion, the confidence to take the leap of faith and pursue change or a dream in your life, is about being 33% planned, prepared, and practiced, 33% sure of your success, 33% sure that you will excel at the four characteristics to do what it takes, and 1% the guts to PURSUE. The interesting part is, it's the 1% that holds many people back. I say seize the day! The most incredible thing is that you are in absolute control of your choices, time, money, and people, to pursue. The question is, do you have the ability to adapt, perseverance, a healthy-positive attitude, and the communication skills to do what it takes?

I BELIEVE THAT YOU DO! Everyone is born with the four special characteristics needed to excel in the four areas of choices, money, people, and time. The problem is that life happens, and our bad experiences, the past, and a stream of bad choices get in the way of our success. We dig ourselves into a hole and feel helpless, like it's just too deep to dig our way back out.

Listen, the first choice that you need to make is:

ENOUGH IS ENOUGH and YOU ARE TIRED OF YOUR CIRCUMSTANCES. Look above your current circumstances and make the choice to make new and better choices for your life. How do you think homeless people become rich, poor people become successful, kids surrounded by horrible circumstances break through and become successful in life? It's because they make a choice to PURSUE a better life. Remember, you don't drown by falling into the water…you drown by staying there.

You've heard some of my story in each of the previous chapters. I've been through a lot in my life. I've been unemployed, I've wondered if I even had enough money to put food on the table for my family, I've had two friends chip in to pay my mortgage payment, I've experienced the pain of divorce…TWICE, and I've drowned in a state of bankruptcy. All of these circumstances in my life came about because I did not pursue the right direction with excellence in my choices, people, money, and time. One, or even all, of them were out of alignment.

I remember the day that I decided, NEVER AGAIN. It was the day I chose to pursue bringing all four of the Pillars in my life into alignment, and pursue the Characteristics, with a never quit attitude. It was the summer of 2005. The JaxMetroLive singles ministry was coming to the end of its three-year run of success, and its time as a full-time venture was ending. It was a moment when I was faced with, "Do I keep running with this opportunity, or make another choice?" Taking my family's needs into consideration, I had probably stayed in the ministry about a year too long. I had become blinded by the emotions that I had birthed this thing, and it was making such a difference in people's lives. Why shouldn't I continue on? However, the reality of it was, it wasn't financially providing for my family's needs. I came to that fork in the road of a good or bad choice. In the summer of 2005, I made the choice to get back into the corporate world. I sat down and went through the thought process I discussed in the Prepare and Practice chapter. Once I got it all down on paper, I was then disturbed enough about my circumstances to begin PURSUING my future.

I jumped, with a huge leap of faith, into pursuing a corporate position. There were only two companies in my city that even did what I was great at and had plenty of experience for. Neither of them had any openings, so I made another good choice, to make another leap of faith and pursue a financial planning career. I had experience with financial planning from early in my work life. I landed a job with a major financial planning company, and within sixty days of working in this new position, I received the call I spoke of earlier in the book, from the one company, in the huge city of Jacksonville, who could offer me a position, in the field that I wanted to enter…and that I was very good at. I made the leap to pursue that opportunity, and I have helped my current company experience growth of over 1,500% since 2006.

What I learned was that once you start pursuing opportunities and pursuing them with excellence, your opportunities in life will change dramatically because people will see you as a doer…someone who makes things happen. By pursuing with a passion to help people, and not to sell them something, people are drawn to help you because you pursue with no agenda to gain something in return. You just want to help.

The moral of this chapter is, don't be afraid to pursue. Seize the moment and go! The ultimate life awaits your arrival. Remember the *Path to the Ultimate Life* visual contains everything that controls your path to your dreams. Look at it often to make sure your obituary won't suck.

APPLICATION TO MAXIMIZE YOUR DASH

What do you fear most about pursuing your dreams?

If everything were in alignment, describe what your ultimate life would look like?

What lessons have you learned now, in the present, from looking back to when you took a leap to pursue big decisions in your past?

What do you think that you should NOT do when pursuing big decisions?

ACTION STEPS TO MAXIMIZE YOUR DASH

Write down the life changing thing that you want to pursue in the next 6 months?

What two steps are you going to take in the next 30 days to pursue the big decision above?

CHAPTER 19

IT'S TIME TO PARTY

"It's your life 'party' that refreshes, reenergizes, and refuels your soul and passion for life. 'Party' your way, and do it often."

WOW! So, you have made it to chapter 19, my favorite chapter…It's Time to Party! This is what this book is really about. You have accomplished so much at this stage of the game. Let's look at what you have learned so far:
- The four primary things that will impact every deci-

sion you make to live the ultimate life
- The four characteristics you need to have to excel in those four areas of decision-making
- You are your own Chief Energy Officer
- You own your decisions and your future
- You have defined your purpose
- You have discovered your passions
- You have defined your principles to live by
- You have set your priorities in order
- You have surrounded yourself with the right people
- You've discovered how to become FREE of your past
- You have planned the path that you want to take
- You have prepared and practiced for your success
- You have paused and meditated on your plan
- You have made the leap to pursue and succeed

That is such an amazing accomplishment to have worked through all of that for your life! NOW IT'S TIME TO PARTY AND CELEBRATE the victories, freedom, and ultimate life you will be experiencing along the way! Now, before you run off and say, "Now Tom, I'm not the partying type" or, "Tom, I'm over forty years old. I gave up partying years ago." Let me define partying for you. My definition of partying is "Doing that which gives you the most fulfillment to refuel, reenergize, and refresh your life to keep up the pursuit of your purpose and passions for the ultimate life."

For some, that may be reading a novel on a beach somewhere. For someone else, it may be taking a cruise. For others, it may be hiking through the Grand Canyon. For my wife and I, we love a good cruise with a great nightclub on it. We love camping, biking, and hiking. We love great music and dancing. Dancing allows us to let loose of energy, while also feeding our souls with a good time, doing what we love. We also love the opportunities that a cruise provides to see many unique places in one travel experience. You can experience and see so many amazing things and meet new people. That is what feeds us as a couple and refreshes us to meet the demands that we have chosen with our life goals.

If you want your obituary to not suck, then you need to find what your party is and do it often. People from all types of life and personalities are drawn to people who know how to enjoy life at any level. If you are not a people person, I would encourage you to get out of your comfort zone, find your "party", and experience it with others who enjoy the same "party" as you. You can leverage your party activity to expand your network of people who could expand your life opportunities, or your talents can help to expand theirs. Remember, the ultimate life is as much about giving as it is receiving.

So, what is your "party"? Have you discovered it? If you haven't, you need to find out what your "party" is and seek to do it now and do it as often as time and money allows. Doing your "party" will refresh your soul. It will provide enjoyment, happiness, and a level of positive energy that nothing negative can penetrate into your life. Will negative things come into your life? Absolutely, misery loves company, but it will not dictate your life. When your glass of life is so full of positive things and emotions, there is no room for negative things.

I have sat and talked with so many people in my life, and I hear this common theme, "I can't wait to retire to start pursuing my passion in life." I see so many people who are living to work, when they should be working to LIVE! Remember, work is simply the financing mechanism that brings the funding for you to pursue the things that you enjoy the most. If you are not able to pursue them right now, and you would like to, then you need to go back to the ***Path to the Ultimate Life*** visual and study it. Work through your choices, money, people, and time decisions, to put you on a path to being able to do "your party" on a regular basis, so you can experience life today.

If you need a motivator to start now, go back to the life exercise and look at how many white blocks you have left. If you are younger, don't wait until there aren't many left to decide to live your life. If you are older, get moving now. Every day you wait is another set of blocks being colored in, without you experiencing the life you desire to have.

Another step that I want you to take as you pursue your "party", is to take pictures…and take a lot of them as you visit amazing places and enjoy incredible experiences with amazing people. Each year, look back at your year of pictures and rejoice in those experiences, the people you have met, the fun you have had, and the memories you've created. Technology has played a huge role in our lives, in being able to see everyday, the incredible moments that we regularly enjoy. There are online programs called Printagram and PosterMyWall, that in a few short steps will allow you to select a 20" x 30" poster, upload 50+ pictures from your Instagram or Facebook account, and have a glossy, high quality poster mailed right to your house.

This past year, my wife and I created two posters with the pictures of us over the past two years, and a poster of our favorite pictures of our kids. We hung those three posters on our wall going up our stairs to our bedroom, so that every time we go up or down the stairs, we are looking at the most incredible experiences that we have had over the last two years. We have committed to changing one out each year to update the wall and keep it fresh. Staying consistently happy throughout your life is about being able to remember the good times you have had and smile at them on a bad day to remind you that your life really is good. One bad day or experience doesn't define your life…don't let it.

You see, we get burned out in life because we can come to a place where we forget that our life is really pretty good. Having the visual documentation on the walls that you pass by every day helps you to remember how awesome your life really is, and the people in it will keep you on fire, wanting to experience more of life. That is why programs like Facebook and Instagram are so amazing… they document and touch on the positive emotions that you have experienced, so that you can go back and see that life is really pretty good.

Since PosterMyWall allows you to upload pictures from any of your friends Facebook photo galleries, you can document a friend's set of amazing life events as well, and have it mailed directly to them as a gift. We had a poster designed in a matter of minutes, documenting a friend's previous two years of their best Facebook pictures, and had it delivered to their new place as a house warming gift. You would have thought we had given them a million dollars. They loved it because it brought back so many great emotions and memories of the past year that this couple spent together. They loved it so much that they put it on the wall right by their front door, so they could see it every day…coming in and out of their house.

A big key to having an awesome life, is remembering consistently how awesome your life has been up to that moment. Without the cool experiences being shown to us, on a constant basis, we can easily lose sight of how exciting our life actually is.

Make a commitment to find your "party." Document it with pictures and/or videos and use them in a way that helps you to remember how great your life is. Don't leave them on your camera or in a computer folder or put them in some album that will never be opened. Share those photos in such a way that you stay tuned into how good the "party" of your life really is.

If your pictures and memories are ones that you would prefer to leave behind, then go back to my *Path to the Ultimate Life* visual and rethink how you need to change your decisions, money, time, and people. Start making a poster of pictures today that you would love to have hanging on your wall, making you smile every time you pass it.

Refresh, refuel, and reenergize your life today. Don't let a spot on your chest, a bad mammogram, a sudden heart attack, or a life altering accident be the reason that you decide to find your "party." Find it starting today and do it often. Find others who enjoy the same "party" and experience it with them. Your health, your soul, and your future obituary will thank you for it years later.

APPLICATION TO MAXIMIZING YOUR DASH

What is your "party" that refreshes, refuels, and reenergizes your life?

What keeps you from experiencing your "party" as much as you would like?

How often do you feel you need to experience your "party" to keep your life refreshed, refueled, and reenergized?

What changes do you need to makc to start experiencing your "party" this week?

ACTION STEPS TO MAXIMIZING YOUR DASH

Write down the changes you will make this week toward pursuing your "party."

Write down how many times you are going to commit to experiencing your "party" over the next year.

CHAPTER 20

THE POWER OF NETWORKING

"Every hand you shake has the power to change your life."

The power of networking can transform your personal life, career, and business, if you take the time to master what it's all about. In my opinion, networking is one of the greatest life skills never taught to us as children or business professionals, yet we are called upon daily to do it all the time. Every day, both personally and professionally, we have opportunities and challenges that are presented to us. Each day, people who could enhance those opportunities, or bring a solution to our challenges, walk into our lives. Most people never even know how others can help them, because they never bother to engage them in a conversation that would lead them to know how they can help. With networking, most conversations are never about if someone can help you right now. Most conversations are about getting to know someone, and then remembering what you have learned about them in your mental database, for that moment of time in the future when they can help you or someone you know.

Networking, as defined by Webster Dictionary, is "a supportive system of sharing information and services among individuals or groups having a common interest." Today, we live in a personal and business climate, in which the demands on us as individuals, can be almost overwhelming. It moves at light speed; change is constant, and the ability to keep up with it all seems impossible. With this fast-paced and changing environment, in a world where we can never really "know it all", why would you try to go it alone?

The first key to any advancement or growth in personal life, professional development, or business, is surrounding yourself with a constantly growing network of people who can provide you or your organization with help, at any given time. It's what this entire book is about. To build a network of people effectively, you have to understand the art of networking.

The way to build a network is not about entering into a conversation to see what someone can do for you. The first step in networking is to get to know people and see how you can help them. Through that conversation, they will ultimately share how they may be able to help you in some way.

I had the fortunate pleasure of attending a conference a few years ago, where I heard an amazing speaker. She has an amazing story about how learning and using the art of networking helped her to rise through the ranks, from a 19-year-old intern at the White House, to the White House Director of Events and Meetings at age 25. Ultimately, she was producing every event that President Clinton was involved with. She stated over and over, that while she was working her way up through the ranks, whenever she would enter any social event and meet people, her number one question was, "How can I help you?" I've learned quickly that when people get to know you over time, they size you up, trying to gauge whether or not you are a taker or giver. If people brand you as a "giver," then they want to be around you more, because you aren't seen as someone always wanting something from them. If you are deemed a "taker," people don't necessarily make an effort to hang with you or want to help you, because they feel like you will ask them for something. In your connections with people, make sure you are a "giver of life," not a "taker of life." People WANT to help givers.

In the world of networking, people will always remember those who have helped them to be successful, and typically, they are more than willing to return the favor. The key to this element is, that you give to help them achieve their goal without expectation of the return favor…that makes it genuine.

As I stated earlier, networking is about a connection to an individual or group of people who, through your positive relationship, can help you at any given moment in time. The first key to focus on is the "positive" relationship. Most people don't like to be around people who bring a negative emotion to the relationship. People like to help people who are bringing a positive vibe; that make progress going forward in life or business. No one enjoys listening, in any kind of meeting, to the person who always says… "Well that's not going to work and let me tell you why it won't work." I'm not saying that no one should ever question something, but there are people who question everything for the purpose of keeping things the way they are, or out of fear of change. These are people that you want to steer clear of. They are disruptive to your life and progress in achieving your goals. That's not to say that you never hang out with them…you just don't bring them into your inner circle that is helping you to meet your life or business goals.

The second key is "the connection" to an individual or group of common interest. Networking is all about the connection and commonality. There are two types of connections: a connection to you, and a connection between that person and someone you know, who could use their expertise. I have gained more favor in life within my network by being a master connector. When I'm talking to people, I always get their business card. As I talk to them, I write down on their card how they may help someone I know someday. I make sure that I put them in my personal database, so they are always in my phone. As life happens, and people around me talk about opportunities or challenges happening, people love it when you are able to say, "Hey, I know this person who can help you. Let me connect you two tomorrow and see how they can help." Their eyes light up and they get a big smile. This is especially true if it's a business referral. Leverage the fundamentals of networking from this chapter to help yourself, but more importantly, how to connect people who need each other.

The key to building your network is in your common interests or needs. The common areas of interests or needs are important, because it gives you the basis of something to get to know each other around. If you have nothing in common, the conversation will be short. In networking, you want to focus on areas that allow for depth of conversation, so you can get to know someone well.

I heard a phrase once that changed my life with regards to relying on people and building trust. It goes like this:
- You should never trust someone more than you know them.
- You should never rely on someone more than you can trust them.
- You should never commit to someone more than you can rely on them.

I see people every day who trust someone with something important when they barely know them. I see people who rely on others way more than they can trust them, and they commit to people who they can't rely on very much. It is important for the success of your life that you pay close attention to the three statements above. Make sure you really know someone as much as you trust them, can rely on them as much as you trust them, and never commit to someone that you can't rely on.

When it comes to looking at the common areas to build your network, some groups to think about are:
- Those with similar interests
- Individual with similar needs
- Same age range
- Mentors
- Same stages of life (married, single, parents, business owner)
- Career type
- Spheres of Influence

Spheres of influence is a really big one, because these are people who know many people, and are influential within their network. A key strategy within online social networking, is to not necessarily have 10,000 average followers, but to have 100 highly influential followers who have 10,000 followers of their own…that taps you into 1,000,000 people!

The same holds true in your face-to-face network, as well as, building a network of individuals you know. You should build a network of people who will open up other networks for you.

Another major key to networking is to know your personality and the personalities of others. To maximize your success at networking, you need to take the time to understand the strengths and weaknesses of the four different personality types. The most successful networkers that I've ever experienced have always been able to identify what makes people tick within minutes of talking to them. Knowing this allows them to know "how" to talk to people. Some people want to hear your vision…some want to hear about your family…some want to hear the bottom line. Everyone has a way to talk to them that causes them to engage in your presence the most. Think about it. It's like walking into a room full of people who speak different languages. If you walk over to a group of four people who speak Chinese and you are trying to speak English, you aren't going to get very far. However, if you begin to speak Chinese to them, you draw an instant connection with them that brings them closer to you. The same holds true with personality types. If you have someone who puts a lot of focus on the details of a situation, and you start talking about a big vision, then you've lost them. If you have someone who is a quiet type and very personal, and you start prying into them with overly personal questions, then you've lost them.

The more you can understand about who people are, it will help you to know "how" to talk to them to get them to open up and draw them closer to you. There are many resources and books that you can access to study the four personality types. I would recommend tapping into them soon. With that said, lets take a brief look at the four personality types.

The four personality types have all been characterized in many ways, including Greek words, shapes, animals, and colors. They all break down to four:

- Life of the Party
- Decision Maker
- Perfectionist
- Can't We All Just Get Along

Here is a short list of strengths and weaknesses of each personality type:

LIFE OF THE PARTY

- **Strengths:** Talkative, Energetic, Creative, Starts Everything, Lives in Present
- **Weaknesses:** Exaggerates, Undisciplined, Doesn't Listen Well, Doesn't Follow Through

DECISION MAKER

- **Strengths:** Born Leader, Goal Oriented, Delegates Well, Can Run Anything
- **Weaknesses:** Bossy, Impatient, Manipulative, Knows Everything

PERFECTIONIST

- **Strengths:** Deep Thoughts, Persistent, Sacrifices for Everyone, Loves Analysis Work

- **Weaknesses:** Not People Oriented, Critical of Others, Sees the Negative, Not a Very Tactful Communicator

WHY CAN'T WE ALL JUST GET ALONG

- **Strengths:** Easy Going, Consistent, Avoids Conflict, Good Listener
- **Weaknesses:** Not Self Motivated, Avoids Responsibility, Resists Change, Would Rather Watch

Everyone typically has one personality type that is their dominating style, with a secondary style that compliments it. I found my personality types in my early thirties, when I had just moved in with a new roommate. One day he came home and shared that he had just taken this personality test and he shared it with me. He said it would be interesting for me to take one to see how our lifestyles might clash. At first, I was hesitant, but a few days later I clicked the link and took the test. When I got the instant result, I was astonished and shocked. It stated that I was the "Life of the Party" type with "Decision Maker" tendencies. When I read through the one-page summary description of my personality traits it freaked me out. It said I was "Captain Wild Child"; starts everything but finishes nothing; disorganized and talks a lot. These were just a few of the many descriptions. I was like... "THIS IS ME AND I'M IN TROUBLE!"

It was very important for me at this very moment in my life to learn this, because I had just landed my first CEO position with a non-profit trade association, in charge of three companies with over $3,000,000 in annual revenue and $4,000,000 in the bank. I basically said to myself, "If I don't make some changes in myself, I'll be fired in the first year."

You see, it is important to look in the mirror at yourself and your personality, so you can learn who you are at the core of your being. The biggest mistake anyone makes is saying, "That personality test is a lie. That's not me." What you are saying is, "I don't like who I am." If you want to be all that you can be in life, then you need to be real with who you are. This will help you to make the changes in your life that are needed to strengthen the areas that will hold you back or make you someone that people don't want to listen to or be around.

After reading the report, I immediately analyzed myself and implemented changes to help me be more effective in life such as: I started using a day timer and checklists to ensure that I don't forget details, I made sure to not say a word until someone finished their story, and I try not to start any projects unless there are resources and time available to do them effectively. I looked in the mirror, took ownership of who I was, and made changes to help me be more effective and successful in life. I will admit, even today, I'm not perfect in these areas, but I'm a work in progress. If you are not careful, your natural weak tendencies will come out of nowhere. It's why I have always surrounded myself with people who have strengths in my areas of weakness.

When looking at personalities, you need to discern whether the traits that you, or anyone else has, is a natural trait, or a learned trait. Natural traits are typically your strengths that you do with no problem. Learned traits are things that you have done to strengthen your weaknesses as I stated above. I am naturally a disorganized person. If you looked at how I manage my life, you would think I'm a very organized person. Organization is a learned trait for me. The goal is to leverage the strengths that you have naturally and learn how to strengthen your areas of weakness. If you do play to your strengths and improve on them, or hire people for your weaknesses, you will be a person who will be successful in many areas of your life.

When I talk about these various personality traits with others, the first thing they say to me is, "Wow. Now I know why he or she reacts this way when I do this." When you know someone's personality traits, it will help you to understand why they respond or react in a certain way, given your interaction with them. This helps you to act, or communicate in a way, so people will hear what you need them to hear.

Let me give you an example that I've personally witnessed. Let's say you are a "life of the party" type like me, who can more or less "wing it" during the workday. You can run with little organization, but not too much. You are always flexible and can react instantly when people put things on your desk to do. Let's say you work with a "perfectionist", who is highly organized with their day…everything has its place and will get done as it comes up on their written schedule. If you walk into the "perfectionist's" office and drop a project of any type on their desk that has to be done sooner rather than later, that situation is not going to go down well. Not because they don't want to, or can't get it done, but because you gave it to them in a way that totally conflicts with their personality. To effectively fit into their mind-set, you should have walked in and asked them if they had some time to help you on a project, talk to them about when they might be able to discuss it, and then get the project on their calendar to go over it and plan it out. Doing that, you just spoke their "language", and they respected you for it, as well as, responded very favorably.

You see, the reason many people don't respond well to someone's requests isn't because they dislike you. They just don't like the way that you treat or ask them, because you don't respect their time and space by speaking in their "personality language." We tend to speak and treat people like we are talking to someone who thinks and acts just like us... big mistake. You have to talk to people in a way that they understand what you are wanting to communicate and asking them to do.

The last key is to understand that networking is continuous and perpetual...it never stops. Every time you enter a room or shake a hand, it's an opportunity to meet someone who may be the connection that you need for a job, a referral, or help getting in the next door. In every social situation, there is someone in the room that you need to meet that you do not know.

I know what many of you are saying at this point, "But Tom, I'm not a people person. I'm uncomfortable in a room full of people, especially people I don't know." Let me assure you that many people you may meet in that room also feel the same way. So, my encouragement to you is to step out of your comfort zone and introduce yourself. At the end of this chapter, I will share a simple system for you to use, on how to start up and move a conversation forward with anyone.

A few other keys that you need to note on being a power networker are:

Be Viral

A ton of networking and connection takes place online with LinkedIn, Facebook, Instagram, SnapChat, and Twitter. I've heard stories of someone seeing six-figures of business come their way, simply because they sent a positive tweet to the CEO of a company whose product they used. The CEO responded back, and the next thing you know, they connected, and they are now seeing business from that company. Had they called the CEO, they would never have gotten past the receptionist, but Twitter and other social media tools allow you to bypass the gatekeeper and be heard by everyone.

Minimize and Eliminate Time Wasters

Your time is valuable, and while you are talking to someone who has no interest in who you are, you are missing out on connecting with someone who may be a vital connection to your life. Remember, there are people who network simply to empty their bucket of drama on others and talk about other people. Minimize your quality time with these people.

Listen with Your Heart...Often

Simply put, be genuine and hear people's stories. Don't fake who you are. Be real and transparent. When you open up your heart to people and listen to theirs, that is when the ultimate connections are made.

Always be Aware of Where You Are, Who You Are With, and Who Could Be Watching

There's a time and place for everything. In the world of networking and video phones in every hand, you want to make sure that you aren't letting your hair down in an environment that could have negative consequences to some future opportunities that you may have. Almost anything you do out in the open, and sometimes behind closed doors, will be documented by someone standing from afar with their phone...next thing you know, you are a feature on the internet. Be wise to not do something that, if seen by many in the open space, would have a big negative impact on your personal life or career.

Be Curious

Ask lots of questions and get to know others. People LOVE to talk about themselves, what they do for a living, their family, and hobbies. They love to brag about themselves. Leverage that to your advantage. Share your wisdom when asked, but only when asked. Always ask people for permission to give them feedback. Don't force your opinions and help people to create ideas and solutions. Don't be afraid to challenge ideas.

Remember and Use Names

People love to hear other people call them by name. If you don't think so, try saying, "Thank you (INSERT NAME)", the next time you purchase something. You will see the person smile. Calling someone by name says, "You were important enough for me to remember your name." This is especially true when you meet someone for the first time and don't see them again for a while. When, on the next interaction, you immediately call them by name, that's very impressive to them. A good idea is to get a picture with them and their business card and upload their information into your phone with a picture of their face for future reference. Use technology in networking to help you be impressive.

Not Everyone Will Like You

Remember that we are all different. Not everyone likes or gets along with certain personalities. There are differing opinions. Many people have a past that just won't allow them to like who you are, and some are going to be jealous or envious of you for whatever reason. Getting along with others takes grace, patience, and forgiveness. I will say this though, if numerous people consistently don't like you, have negative things to say about you, and you are always on the outside looking in, then you need to take a look in the mirror.

You may need to make some personal adjustments as we spoke about before. However, if a small percentage of people in your life don't like you, don't let it deter you...move on, they are most likely time wasters. My motto is, if 10% of the people in your life are not indifferent to who you are and what you stand for, then you probably aren't growing, innovating, and pushing the envelope enough...you are just trying to make everyone happy and go with the crowd. You are not called to make everyone happy...you are called to make a difference.

Everybody is Somebody

Always assume that you need to meet a person. Never underestimate who you are shaking hands with. That person could know the person who is your next boss or next big client. Always treat everyone you meet with respect and honesty, as if they are the person who knows someone else you need to meet.

Business cards

Like the American Express commercial says... "Never leave home without it." Business cards are how people remember you once you leave their presence. As you develop your business cards, think about having a QR code so people can scan it with their phone...this way you are in their phone immediately. If you are unemployed, a college student, or working for a company who doesn't provide you with business cards, then have some made up for yourself with your contact information on them and your own "self title." The best one that I ever saw was a friend of mine who gave herself the title, "Your Go-To Girl." She was saying to anyone that she gave her card to, "If you need something, I can help." That's creative and memorable to anyone that she gives that card to.

Now that you know the keys to networking, I want to share with you a simple system for connecting with people once you have entered the room. It's a nice mental system of networking communication that I learned from a colleague who has since passed on. As you approach someone at the bar, networking event, church event, or small group, you have just reached out your hand and said typically, "Hi, my name is…." Most people don't know what to say next. Here is what should come next…it's called F.O.R.M.:

FAMILY

Everyone likes to talk about their family, so you start with simple questions like:
- Where are you originally from?
- Does your family live here?
- How long have you and your wife lived here?
- What are your kids into at their ages?

At some point, you then will transition into:

OCCUPATION

Most people like to talk about what they do, whether it's good or bad, so you move into questions related to their work:
- So, what do you do for a living?
- How is the economy in that industry?
- What are the major challenges a company like yours is seeing right now?
- What do you like the most about your job?

RECREATION

People have passions or outside activities that they love:
* When you aren't at work, what do you like to do?
* What do you like best about that activity?
* Are you a sports fan?
* Who is your favorite team?

MY TIME

After talking with someone about their Family, Occupation, and Recreation, now it's **"MY TIME."** The problem (not really a problem) is that you never get to "MY TIME" because you spent so much time letting the other person do what they like to do most…talk about themselves.

Your letting them talk so much about themselves, leaves them thinking that you are this incredible listener, and an awesome person that they just met. BOOM! Connection and lasting impression made.

Again, networking is a life skill everyone should master. Start working on your ability to connect. You never know which hand you shake that will change your life forever in the future. I have a book full of stories about how people I met through networking have helped my life, or I have connected people who have helped each other. A hand I shook in 1995, called me in 2005 to ask me if I would come be his #2 person in his company, to eventually take over as CEO when he retired in two years. He said, while interviewing me, he always remembered how passionate my ideas were when he met me 10 years earlier…I was his only call to be his #2 person. That is the power of networking. Learn to be a power networker and connector of people, and those around you will help you in a way over time that will make your obituary not suck.

APPLICATION TO MAXIMIZING YOUR DASH

What do you fear most about networking with people you don't know?

What personality type are you?

What do you feel are your strengths and weaknesses as a person, professional, and a friend?

What personality type rubs you the wrong way?

What are the areas that you need to improve on to help you be a more effective networker and connector of people?

ACTION STEPS TO MAXIMIZING YOUR DASH

Make a list of people you need to network with and groups you need to join.

Take a personality test to find out who you are.

Look at your list of strengths and weaknesses and make a list of action steps to help you strengthen your areas of weakness.

Order your business cards if you don't have any.

Commit to networking at least once a month with some group in your local area.

CHAPTER 21

YOUR PEOPLE MUST BE DIVERSE

"To maximize your opportunities and quality of life, it's important that you open up to diverse groups of people at all levels. Everyone has something good to offer in your life."

We all know that the talk of diversity brings with it a ton of emotions, politics, and differences in opinion. This chapter is not going to seek to solve all of the socio-economic issues that exist that drive the discussion of diversity. What it is going to focus on is the human element of diversity.

As we come upon diverse groups of people, we all have a choice to be respectful and treat people with human decency…no matter who they are, or you can treat them as if they are different. That is where the hate, and negative things that occur with diversity CAN come into play. I'm going to encourage everyone reading this book to see everyone that you meet in life as being just like yourself. Treat them like another human being and respect their differences. Treat them as you would want them to treat you. Understand that they too are someone's son, daughter, father, or mother. They are a human being first and foremost.

All you have to do to see diversity is watch television, walk outside, or read any number of magazines. Our society today is a melting pot of people. People who think, act, and speak differently. Diversity comes in many shapes, sizes, and colors. If you live the average life span of 79 years old, you are going to experience people of many religions, skin colors, genders, ages, nationalities, and each with their own unique thought processes.

They all bring a different skill set, skill levels, opinions, and opportunities to your life. It is very important for you to know that you need to build a life of diversity if you are to achieve a great quality of life. To see the diversity, take a look at the latest 2010 census data of the population of the United States:

Gender (U.S.):
51% Male
49% Female

Age (U.S.):
34%   Under 18

30%	25 - 44
23%	45 - 65
13%	65 +

Ethnic Groups (U.S.):

72%	White American
13%	African Americans
4.8%	Asian Americans
1.0%	Native Americans
0.2%	Native Hawaiian
6.2%	Some other ethnic group

Religion (World)

32%	Christian
23%	Islam
16%	Unaffiliated
15%	Hinduism
7%	Buddhism
6%	Fold Religions
1%	Other

My point of sharing this data is to show you, that we no longer live in a world where there is one kind of people who think, live, or act the same way. You live in a country, as well as, a world that is very diverse. You need to learn to be open to other people's thinking and ideas. That doesn't mean that you accept their thinking, it simply means that you understand that not everyone thinks like you, and that you respect others' rights to think differently. Remember, there are a lot of people all around you who look at you thinking the same thing you think about them... "I can't believe he/she thinks like that!"

By becoming more accepting of a diverse set of people in your life, it frees you to explore other cultures, other ways of thinking, and a more stress-free life.

Instead of looking at someone as being different, because of their religion, gender, or skin color, remember that they have a family just like you. They have a mother. They have a father. They may have kids. They have friends. They work for a living. Most importantly, they are a human being, who is just trying to make it in this world…just like you. Just because they don't look, act, or think like you, doesn't make them worse than you, it just makes them different.

Being a different skin color, religion, or nationality shouldn't be a reason for you to disengage someone from your life. You need to be welcoming and engaging to everyone around you. Those you should think about disengaging in your life, should be those who don't stand for the same positive principles that you have in your life, and those who bring a negative impact on your life in one of the four key areas of: choices, money, time, and people you hang with.

I encourage you not to judge people on first sight but get to know their story. Everyone has a story, and a path of decisions that have brought them to any given moment in life. Everyone has a past, filled with good and bad experiences, that have shaped their life up to this point. If a particular person is down on their luck, or is close to giving up hope, they may need someone just like you to enter their life, to empower them, and speak truth and hope into their life.

I've witnessed many people in my own life who made prejudgments about people before they were able to actually meet them. Once they got to know who they are, and what their life story was, they had a totally different opinion of them.

Don't let diversity cause you to be a divider of people. Let it cause you to be a lover of people of all types, that brings them together for good. Remember my chapter on networking? Take that chapter and use it as a guide to reach out and get to know others in your local community or industry that aren't like you. As your network of diverse people in your life grows, you will see your life begin to grow.

APPLICATION TO MAXIMIZING YOUR DASH

What do you fear about being around people who aren't like you?

What were you told by your parents about people who aren't like you? Do you still believe them?

If you were to look at 100 people you see over the course of a year, are they a diverse group in age, color, religion, nationality, or thinking?

Why do you feel people are so divided over the differences in others?

ACTION STEPS TO MAXIMIZING YOUR DASH

Take the time to expand your network into a new diverse group of people within the next 30 days.

Write down three things that you need to change about your thinking to help you create more people diversity in your life.

CHAPTER 22

IDENTIFY YOUR THREATS TO YOUR QUALITY OF LIFE

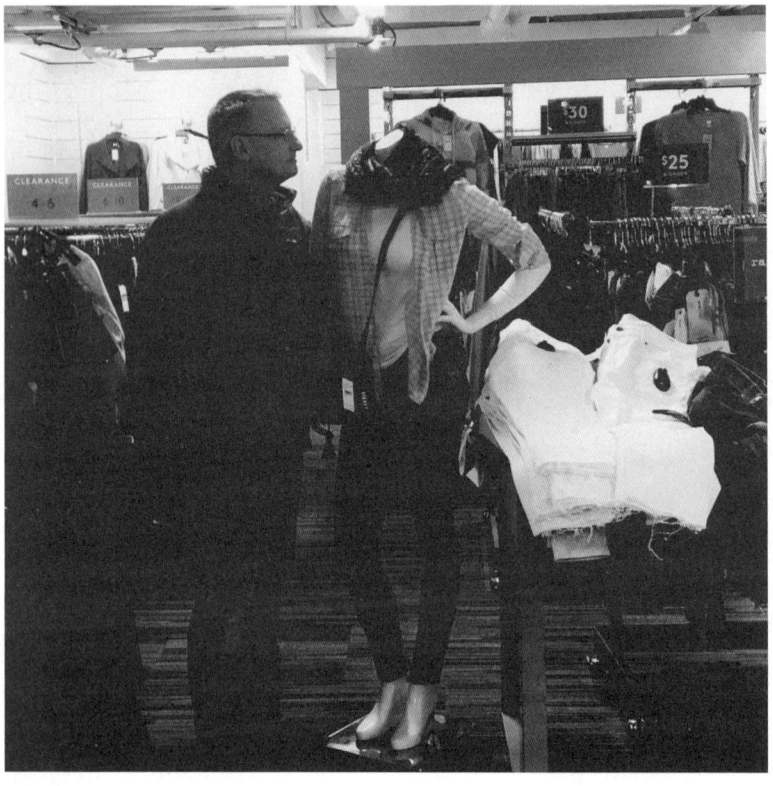

"No matter what goals you are pursuing in life, there will always be threats to your success. Almost every threat can be prepared to minimize its impact on your success."

Most people wouldn't spend the time thinking about the threats to the quality of life that they are striving for. Threats are typically things that you do not see coming, because you aren't looking for them. Yet most every threat to your quality of life, can typically be seen, and in a lot of cases prevented, or at least minimized. That doesn't mean that they can always be prevented, but if you can identify a threat before it has the opportunity to manifest itself, then you can have a plan in place to minimize its impact on your life.

When most people decide on a goal, or purpose they want to obtain, they just decide and go without much thinking on what could prevent their goal from happening. Along the way they incur numerous frustrating obstacles that are speed bumps in their plan. Frustration occurs from not having thought through the path that you are taking to reach your goal and asking, "Along my journey, what will be all the obstacles from people, or unforeseen events that will get in my way?" Asking this question is important, because if you know the obstacles that will get in your way, then you don't see the world as working against you, because you know these things are most likely going to occur.

So, as you look at your situation, where you are in life, and where you are headed, what are all of the threats that can keep you from meeting your goals on time? You need to think for a few moments about threats on any major decisions in your life, including:

- Job changes
- Interviewing for a job
- Getting married
- Having a child
- Having another child
- Dating someone
- Dating again (if divorced or single)
- Going on a big family vacation

These, and many other goals in your life, have the opportunity to derail, or not even occur because of unforeseen events that take place in the process. The reason they are not seen coming, is because you didn't take the time to think about what can happen along the way to your goal. What could prevent it from happening like you want? You need to think about that. Think about it with people close to you, who know where you want to go, and have some life experience in that area. Write down any event, good or bad, that could prevent or derail your goal. Then, start thinking through solutions to ensure that you minimize or eliminate their impact.

My wife and I sit down, at least every quarter over dinner, and walk through the conversation of threats on any number of goals in our life. Whether it's a vacation, investing money, or plans in our business, we chat consistently about "What are we not thinking of that can get in the way of our plans?"

I will use as an example, the element of retirement, because it is probably one of the most important goals in life that anyone should have at any age. That's right…any age. Why? Because as I said in my Planning chapter, if you take 100 people at age 25, and look at them when they are 65 years old, 66% of them will have become reliant on other people again for housing, transportation, food, and healthcare. They have lost their independence. Think about it… you graduated college at some point, or began working in your career, and you work all your life to get to 65, and you end up having little to live on. Most people end up this way because no one ever had the serious conversation with them about the "threats" to their plan for retirement. There are life events, as well as people, that will happen in your life that will keep you from saving enough money to one day have the choice to just sit back and enjoy the fruits of your life-long labor.

When you finish reading this book, I never want you to say later in life at retirement, "How did I get to this point?" Retirement is a decision that is fully impacted by the items in four ***Paths to the Ultimate Life***, as I discussed previously, and seen below:

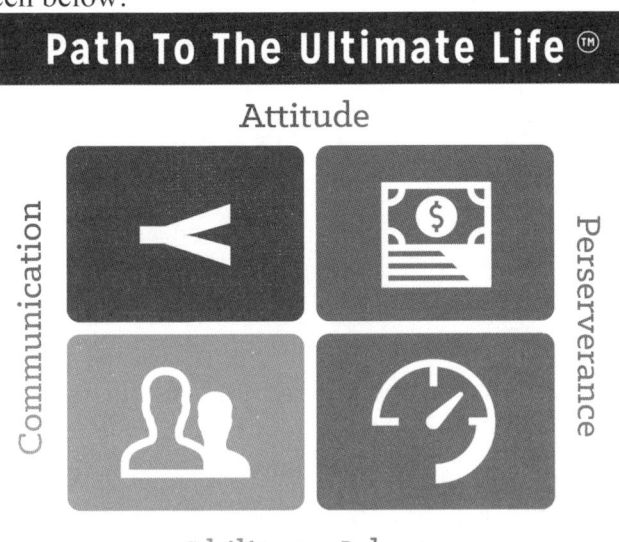

Path To The Ultimate Life ™

Attitude

Communication

Perserverance

Ability to Adapt

In your life, the four things that will keep you from retiring will be your decisions, how you spend/invest your money, time spent planning, and the people you surround yourself with. I didn't figure this all out until I was in my late 40s. I can remember sitting down one day, looking out to age 65, and asking myself, "What will my life be like when I'm within reach of 65?" I see so many people who are in their late 50s, who will not retire with a good standard of living, because they didn't plan or think through the threats to their retirement. Other thoughts that go through my head are:

- What will my expenses be at retirement?
- How much money will I need on an annual basis?
- How do I plan so I have enough money, so as to not

let my fixed income at retirement, prevent me from doing cool stuff?
•   What types of unexpected financial expenses will
happen after retirement that we need to plan for?

All of these questions were rolling through my mind as I
started looking into how to fully fund our retirement. Oh, did
you hear me right? I said FULLY fund. That means that you
are investing money each month, in a variety of different
ways, to create "buckets of money", so that no one bucket
of money, if you were to lose it, can have a negative impact
on your standard of living at retirement. When you reach
retirement, you need to either be working, or have money
"working for you."

As soon as I started going through this process, I thought
to myself, "I wish someone had told me this when I was
in my early 20s!" You know why? Because I just recently
looked at my earnings record since I was 18, from my online
social security account. Had I started putting just 5% of my
gross pay away each year from age 25 to age 65, at a reasonable mutual fund interest rate, I would have $1,200,000
at age 65 to retire on. That was from only putting away 5%.
If you plan and prepare, almost everyone can learn to live
without 5% of your income to prepare for the future. This
doesn't even count any money that your company may invest in retirement for you. For this reason, I encourage anyone who works for a company that has a matching fund retirement program, to maximize the amount they will match.
Years later, you will be loving life, while watching your pot
of money grow.

The moral of this story is, no matter how old you are,
start thinking about how much you need at retirement, to live
the quality of life that you want to live, and start saving AS
SOON AS POSSIBLE.

The second moral, is to think in terms of "buckets of money." When we walked through our plan, we decided we would have a small bucket, coming from social security, and larger buckets coming from permanent life insurance, equity investments in mutual funds, and rental income from a vacation property. Between those four buckets, we could fund our lifestyle at retirement. You need to look at your options with a planner, and decide what your buckets of money will be, and start funding them soon. The amount of money it takes to retire goes up dramatically as you get older.

Now that I've shared our thought process about retirement, let's get back to the discussion of threats to our retiring on time, and having enough money to retire in the fashion that we desire. As my wife and I sat down one night, we started making a list of all the things that could threaten our retirement. They included the following:

- Sudden disability
- Daughter's weddings
- College tuition for children
- Downturn in the economy
- Unexpected death of one of us
- Unforeseen expenses
- Healthcare expenses
- Automobiles breaking and/or needing a new one
- Getting fired or down-sized from a job
- Inability to make monthly investment payments
- Needing to pay for, or care for, a parent when they are older

These are just a few of the many that came up. I bet you saw daughter's weddings and thought, "How is that a threat?" Anything that can deter you from achieving a purpose or goal is a threat…even if it's an awesome and positive event. The reality of it is, weddings are expensive, and if you haven't planned on $20,000 to come out of your savings, or you don't have it, then you may be tempted to tap into your retirement fund to make sure your child has their big wedding day. That can delay retirement, so it is a threat that you need to plan for. Threats are not just negative or bad events. Threats are both good and bad events in your life, that can keep you from reaching your goal on time.

As I stated in my Planning, Preparation, and Practice chapters, the great thing about pre-thinking your threats with any decision, is that you have the time to make a plan to eliminate or minimize their impact. Through my wife and I looking at our threats, we were able to put into place the following solutions:

- Began to market my talents for speaking engagements to earn the extra money that we would need to fund retirement and savings
- Invest in life insurance in case of dying too soon, or living to long
- Start funding an IRA for both of us
- Purchase disability insurance, in case one of us becomes disabled
- Get annual physicals to find out any health issues, before they become serious, and expensive
- Ensure that our car's oil, and other items, are changed and checked regularly, so no automobile problems come out of nowhere (Auto repairs are way more expensive than oil changes every three months.)
- Put a savings account in place for weddings, college, and unforeseen expenses
- Invest most of our money in investments that aren't driven by the volatility of the stock market

You see, once you have your threats on paper, you can put solutions in place to help minimize the negative impact that events, or people can have on your goals. Having the solutions in your back pocket will guarantee that your obituary won't suck, because when you have solutions already figured out for threats, you are more confident, and free to enjoy life knowing your goals are securely met.

Take threats to your goals in life seriously. Don't wing it. You will save time and money, because you have taken the time to think about the solutions to unforeseen threats to your destination.

APPLICATION TO MAXIMIZING YOUR DASH

What threats do you see getting in the way of your personal goals?

What threats do you see getting in the way of your professional goals?

What outside forces are in your life right now that are making it hard for you to achieve your goals?

ACTION STEPS TO MAXIMIZING YOUR DASH

Write down each threat that you feel could slow down, or prevent you from, achieving your goals, personally and professionally?

Write down the action steps that you must take to minimize the impact of each threat.

CHAPTER 23

YOUR COMMUNICATION STATEGY

"It is crucial that you speak to people in their emotional language, so they will understand what you are saying."

Throughout my entire life, there has been one common theme that I have heard from many people, at many different levels of life and work: Failure, in almost any relationship, in personal or professional life, takes place because of a lack of communication. Knowing this, should be a big clue in life, that you need to have some type of communication strategy that helps you succeed above all others. That is why communication is one of my four key Pillars in the **Path to the Ultimate Life** visual. If you don't know how to openly communicate, you will find life is a struggle in many areas. You will not do well in relationships, friendships, job interviews, or proposals in business, just to name a few. You need to know how to share what is on your mind and how you feel.

If open communication is one of the biggest problems in life for people, and if YOU have a personal communication strategy, then you will have an advantage over all other people around you. If you are skilled in good communication, then I guarantee people will connect with you and you will be heard.

As I stated in the chapter on the Power of Networking, we tend to communicate with people as if we are talking to someone who is just like us. That is a wrong communication style. You are saying one thing, and they are hearing another, because their personality and life experience filters are different than yours. It is important that you understand that everyone gives and receives information in very different styles. This is exactly why email and texting are not always the best means of communication. Both email and texting are emotionless, toneless methods of communication. You can't hear the tone of voice, and you can't see the body language from the person sending the message. Because of this, your message just says what it says, and is open to a multitude of interpretations, which is why it can oftentimes come across as cold or curt and can be misinterpreted. What happens is that the receiver of the text or email, interprets what you are trying to say through their own filter of beliefs and experiences, and many times misinterprets the email or text in a way that can create unnecessary conflict, anger, or hurt feelings. They then fire off a response back, and now you are in this firestorm of texts or emails.

Because of the possibility for misinterpretation, there are a few things that you should never discuss or send over email or texts. They are as follows:

Disagreements: Never try to have a conversation over text or email on a subject of disagreement. You typically respond out of hurt or anger because of something that the other person has said to defend their position. Because people feel much bolder behind a phone or computer screen, they are usually more willing to type in a much harsher statement than they would if they were having the discussion with you face-to-face. If you have a disagreement with someone, write down the key items in bullet point format that you would like to talk about, go somewhere public to keep both parties' emotions in check, and have an open, honest communication about it.

Bad News: This can be anything from resigning from a job, firing someone, breaking up with someone, or relaying the news that a person has passed away. The bottom line is, don't send shock waves through someone's life, by sending them the bad news over a text or email. That person woke up ready to rock the day, and then you decided to send them an email, that within seconds, could have a devastating impact on their life. Take the time to find someone else to go with you and deliver the news in person. Think about what you will say, how you will say it, and the potential reaction of the person so you can help them deal with the news. Some situations, like firing a bad employee, you can't help very much, but you can still encourage them as they leave your company, by helping them to understand "why" they got fired. One of my favorites is the person who breaks up with someone via text. Listen, if you have been in a relationship with someone and have spent intimate moments with them connecting, then have the guts to stand before them and have a conversation with them about breaking up. If you don't have the strength to have that conversation, you are going to be very challenged in life because so many other conversations in life are much more difficult. Bottom line…if it is bad news, and the feelings that the other person is going to feel are hurt or anguish, do it face-to-face.

Negativity: This is another huge no-no. Many friends and couples get caught in this battleground when they are not on the same page or having a disagreement. Because we are more aggressive communicators via text or email, we send hurtful statements that we would not normally send, with the sole purpose of inflicting pain. These statements are like daggers being stuck into someone's chest, and you can't take that stuff back…it's in writing! If you have something negative that you feel about someone, take the steps to sit with them and talk it out.

Big News: Now this one I can go half way on. I think it's a big surprise when I get some exciting news over my text or email. It makes you jump for joy, but sometimes you leave the person all alone in the good news. I think it's okay to send big news via text or an email to surprise someone, but always follow up with a quick phone call to share in the excitement with them. People want to talk about big news. I've sent many texts to my wife and kids saying, "Hey, guess what?" When they respond back "What?", I give them the news, and then call them a few second later. Texts and emails are great ways to set up a face-to-face, or phone call, to celebrate big news, but never leave it to just a text or email to deliver it, that takes away from the excitement of the big news.

Let's talk for a bit about social media. I know that many reading this book probably think that social media is a bad thing in our society. You may be saying, "I don't do Facebook or Instagram, and I don't have a LinkedIn account." All I will say is, you are doing yourself, and those around you, a disservice by not using Facebook or LinkedIn as a communication tool.

What you need to understand about the various social media formats is that they expand your ability to network, reach out, create opportunities, and record some of your greatest moments in life. In this age of digital media, who looks through their photo albums anymore, when you can click a button and check out what just happened in your friends or family's life on Facebook, Instagram, or any other social media site. There is no way that any relative could know so much about their friends and family just by making phone calls. Facebook, Instagram, and other social media sharing tools, allow you to see the exciting things going on in everyone's life that is important to you.

Many will say, "Well if they wanted to share it with me, they can just call me." That's impossible. From their end, they have a mother, father, two brothers, a sister, five aunts, five uncles, grandparents, twelve cousins, and who knows how many hundred friends. A person could make a full-time job out of sitting on the phone and calling everyone that they would love to share the things in their life with. On your end, imagine all of those people I just mentioned above, calling you to share great things happening in their life, as they happened. You would turn your phone off because you don't have the time for all of them to call. Programs like Facebook and Instagram allow you to participate in someone's life in a deep and intimate way, when it's convenient for you. There is no need to catch up at the annual family reunion, because you have seen your far away relative's baby take their first steps as it happened...you saw your sister's son graduate high school, and you were able to see your child's experiences at college. I encourage you to embrace social technologies as a means to help you stay closer to the many people in your circles. You can share in their life events every day, versus looking back at a family reunion saying, "I wish I had more time to spend with them."

I am one of those people who use my social media tools to reach out and send encouraging messages to all of those who are connected to me. I personally use Facebook, LinkedIn, Instagram, Twitter, and Hootsuite. The combination of these programs, allow me to reach thousands of people at my fingertips. Why is this important? I travel the country for business and I see many of the people face-to-face that are connected to me on social media. I have had many people tell me that they might have been having a bad day, when something I posted comes across their news feed on Facebook or LinkedIn, or a fun picture on Instagram, and it makes their day. It brightens the moment or lets them know that no matter what you are going through right now, it will be okay. Most people don't need a solution in the moment, they just want to know that they aren't alone, and that it will eventually be okay. My posts are all about making people know that they aren't alone in this thing called life, and that someone out there cares. Tap into your inner being and seek to reach people for good with social media.

I want to conclude this chapter by talking about some effective keys to communication. One of the biggest mistakes that I've witnessed, and I'm guilty of it, is people choosing to discuss something at the wrong time. Remember my story about walking in and seeing on the white board the three words that you need for effective communication: timing, intent, message. This is so true. There is a time, a tone, and a tact to communicating anything. I'm going to add a fourth word: expectations. So many times we set goals for the other person, because we set in our minds how we believe we want them to react or respond to what we say. When they respond in a totally different way, we freak out. In the area of communications, you need to share your ideas and thoughts, without any expectation as to how the other person is going to respond. Be ready for any response though…not just the one you want to hear, because many times you won't.

When you go to discuss anything with someone, always think through:
- Is this the right time?
- What is my intent in communicating this?
- What do I want them to hear?
- What are my expectations of them?

If you choose the right time, have good intentions, say your message in a way that they hear you, without any real expectations of the outcome, then you will most likely be very successful in getting what you want, or at least be at peace with how things turn out.

When it comes to the "right time" to talk about anything, I know there are a few moments in life that you don't ever want to talk about anything big, or in a disagreement with:
- When you are tired
- When you are hungry
- When you are angry
- Late at night

This is especially true in relationships and business dealings. More couples end up in huge arguments over the smallest things, because one of them is pressing the other late at night. …Bad move. Take a step back and say, "You know what, we shouldn't talk about this while we are tired. Let's sleep on it and talk about it over breakfast." This allows the mind time to rest, and if it is a big deal, you will still want to talk about it in the morning when you are well rested.

Regarding hungry and angry, well those speak for themselves. You just don't want to speak to someone about an issue, that you really need them to hear what is being said, when they are angry. Their minds aren't receptive. When people are hungry they can become irritated due to low blood sugar levels. In my house, we call this HANGRY. Take some time to sit down and do the following:

- Analyze who you are, to know and understand your communication style
- Learn the various personality types from the Networking chapter, to know how you need to address others
- Always be thinking of the four questions that I mentioned in this chapter, on timing, intent, message, and expectations
- Know when NOT to bring up something of importance

If you work on those four key areas, you will learn to be a master communicator, and grow the group of people who will help you maximize your experiences in Your Dash.

APPLICATION TO MAXIMIZING YOUR DASH

Describe your communication style.

Do you utilize the various social media programs? If not, why? If so, how does it help in your relationships?

When communicating, which area do you struggle with the most: timing, intent, message, or expectation. Why?

What do you feel that you need to improve on the most with regards to open communication?

Do you have the patience to not break the four rules of when NOT to talk about something of importance?

ACTION STEPS TO MAXIMIZING YOUR DASH

When you feel negative emotions starting to rise during any important conversation, take a step back, and request that you give the situation a 24-hour break before talking about it again.

The next time you have something important to talk to someone about, write down in bullet point format what you want to communicate.

Write down how you are feeling about what you want to communicate to someone.

CHAPTER 24

BE THE MIRACLE!

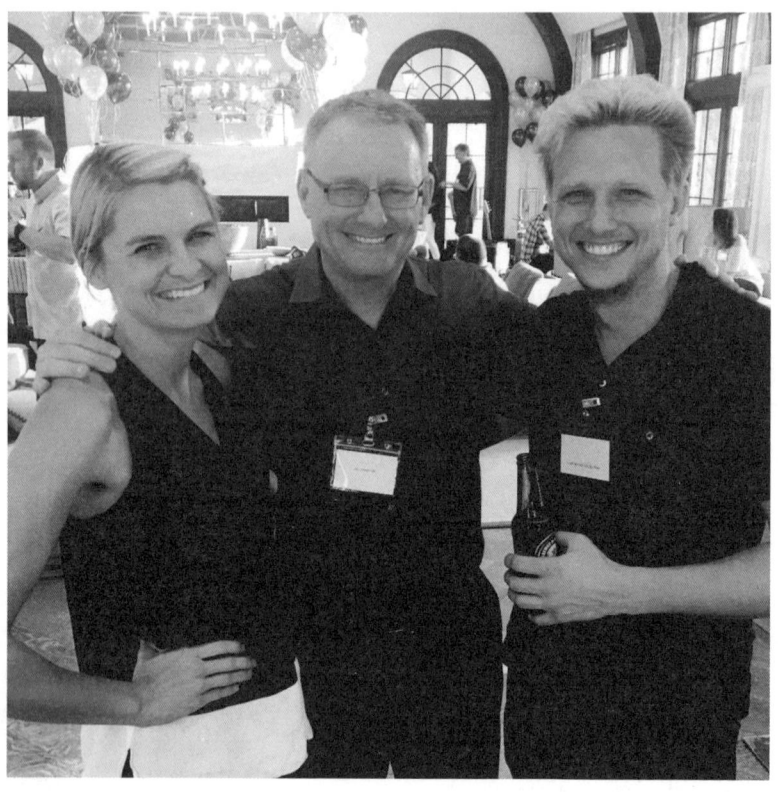

"The more you are the miracle in other people's lives, the more of a miracle that begins to happen in your own life."

For me, this is one of the most important chapters, from a philosophical perspective, for you to grasp. There are a lot of qualities that you need to have, in order to actually achieve the quality of life you want, but there's one quality that will prevent it from becoming reality...let's talk about it:

If you are going to have an obituary that won't suck, you need to be seen as a giver, not a taker when dealing with people. Have you ever been around a taker? Their "What's in it for me" radar is always on when they are around. The questions they ask and the actions they take, tell you that anything they say, ask, or do, for you is all in an effort to get something in return. They aren't about giving anything to you, and people pick up on this very quickly.

People who are givers, with expectation of nothing in return, get more "YES" than "NO" in life, because people see them in a very different light. Do you get "NO" in a lot of your requests of parents, friends, or business colleagues, for things that others are getting a "YES" to? If so, you need to take a serious look at this area. Do you say "NO" to requests often? ...Or are you constantly asking for favors or requests, without ever offering up help. Remember the story about the young White House intern, who worked her way up the ladder by simply asking one question to everyone she met... "How can I help you?" People remember those people, especially if they make a request and you pull it off for them. You are a hero, and they tell others about you.

I love watching the movie, Bruce Almighty, because it sets up this very concept. It actually was life-changing for me, the moment I saw it years ago. I was one of those people who saw the talents I had, and I believed I could be great in whatever industry I worked. As I shared my personality traits earlier, I was a "start everything, hard to finish anything" kind of person. I went at everyone in an effort to help myself be successful, and that attitude didn't work very well. Like Bruce Almighty, I was always praying for a big break...praying for it to walk right into my hands... praying for life to open up, and all my talents and great ideas to take shape. Then one night, I watched Bruce Almighty, and I heard GOD, played by Morgan Freeman, say to Bruce, "Bruce, stop praying for a miracle and be the miracle."

As they say on Facebook, "OMG!" A revelation came flying through my soul. Going back to my *Path to the Ultimate Life* visual, I had to change the choices I was making. By changing my choices, it had a profound impact on my decisions with people, money, and time. The choice that I made, was to "**BE** the MIRACLE" in other people's lives, by focusing in on their needs, wants, and desires, as I spoke or interacted with them. I paid attention to the things that they said seemed to be obstacles, or that were keeping them, from reaching their dreams and purpose. As I listened, I would offer input, or seek to connect them with someone that I knew who could help them. As this began to happen, I began to become more welcoming to people; I saw people's lives reach new levels, because they were introduced to someone by me who could help make their life better. Don't think that miracles have to be huge. Sometimes it is as simple as, needing something small, but in the context of where that person was in life in that moment, me helping to find the solution to that "small thing" on their mind, was a huge deal to them.

A great story that I think about in this context, was with a vendor that we used to have several years ago. I became a close business associate of this person over the years through working with him to better understand our industry. I loved his product and wanted it to be the best for everyone. If it was the best for everyone, then it would be the best for our company as well. After being involved with the product for a couple of months, I knew that they were on the right track. As we were talking at a conference, he indicated that he was looking to go to the next level with his company. I really believed in his vision for his company and being in his late twenties I wanted to see him be a major player in our industry. I leaned over to him and said, "Look, here's the deal. I believe in you, your team, and your product. If you have any clients who are on the fence in the sales process, you give them my email and number, and have them call me. I'll take care of the rest." The look in his eyes was amazement. He was like, "Really? You would do that? How much do I have to pay you in a finder's fee?" My answer, "Nothing. I want to see you do well, and I want my recommendation to be pure, not paid for. Just continue the incredible service and product development that you are doing in your company." I proceeded to take calls over the next few years from potential clients, and within a thirty-minute conversation, slammed the door on the competition for them. I became known as "The Closer" in his company. A number of years later, he landed a nice payday by selling his company to an affiliated company, who was looking to get into his line of work. This was a big day for him in his life. He called me up after the sale and thanked me for being a huge influence on the clients that put him in a position to sell his company. That's being a miracle for someone… reaching out, seizing the moment, using your talents and time, to create life-changing moments for others…with no expectation in return.

One more example of "being the miracle", then we'll move on: I'm pretty active on some industry online forums. I often look through my email notices from the forums, from people who need basic information or connection to someone to help them with a problem or open up an opportunity. I take the time each day to respond to one or two people. I consistently get emails back thanking me for my connection or insight, as it helped save them a ton of time or money. Making a difference and helping doesn't have to take much time or money, it just takes you reaching out and listening.

Never underestimate how big of a deal a problem or opportunity is for someone. What might seem simple or small to you, may be a huge deal in that moment to them, because of the huge checklist of things on their to-do list, or because other people may be putting pressure on them in life. If you are continuing to expand your network of people listed in your phone, then leverage that network to help those that you come into contact with.

You may be asking, "Why be the miracle? I don't like people that much." What I will ask is, for you to remember that feeling when someone reached out to you and took the time to be the miracle in your life. You were in a place where nothing seemed to go right. You were trying everything in your own strength to change your direction, and you felt like your path was riddled with bottomless pits that you kept falling into. Then someone came into your life, at that very moment, and pulled you out of the pit, and gave you a solution or introduced you to a solution, or they just helped you. They walked you around the bottomless pits to the other side of a straight and safe road towards your goal. That feeling of relief was amazing, wasn't it? The internal feeling of excitement, of knowing that the situation is gone, and you can breathe again is incredible. You feel FREE again and are back on the path to good choices…to reaching your goals in life.

Knowing how good it feels when someone reaches out to you, should cause you to want to be the same "miracle" to others who come into your life with the same type of anxiety and challenges. Everyone has talents, experiences, and a network of people that others can benefit from. You need to take a mental inventory of what those are, so you can easily identify when people around you need help.

One thing I want to stress at this point, is in my ***Path to the Ultimate Life*** visual, as you make a CHOICE to be the miracle to others, it will impact your TIME. You can get caught up in saying "YES" to too many people, and it dominates your time, thus preventing you from staying on path to meet your goals and purpose. This is where you need to make a second CHOICE, to learn when to say, "I can't help right now because my glass is full." Learn to know when your glass of energy, emotional presence, and time are full, so you know when to say "no." If you allow your glass of energy, emotional presence, and time to overrun for too long, your attitude will begin to be seen as negative, because you have no PARTY time. You need a way to refresh yourself, to help you stay on track towards your goal of the ultimate life. Are you beginning to see how the various things that I'm talking about in the book are interconnected?

Just by making a choice to be more giving of your time and network could impact your choices, time, money, people, purpose, and party elements. Be wise with them in order to stay on the path toward maximizing Your Dash.

APPLICATION TO MAXIMIZING YOUR DASH

Do you like to help people? Why or why not?

What are your challenges that prevent you from reaching out to people around you in need?

What issues are going on in your life, keeping you from being the miracle for others?

When looking at your choices, money, time, and people, which one do you think you need to focus on in order to be the miracle for others?

ACTION STEPS TO MAXIMIZING YOUR DASH

Write down your own story, about when someone that you didn't expect, reached out and helped you with a challenge or opportunity.

Make a commitment to try and be the miracle for at least two people each month. Look for the "low-lying fruit on the tree." These are people whose needs you can easily help, without dominating your time.

CHAPTER 25

NARROW YOUR FOCUS... DOMINATE YOUR SPACE

"When your life glass of energy and time is overflowing, you have a mess in your life. Learn to narrow your focus and keep your glass of energy and time from spilling everywhere."

As you may have learned throughout this book, up until my early 30s, I was a "start everything" kind of idea guy. I was all over the place looking for that "thing" that could take me to the promised land, make me rich, and accelerate my progress through the stages of life…from entry level management to super-star status, or even early retirement. I was looking for the shortcuts, without all the hard work that comes with obtaining long-term success.

What I have learned is, if you continue to grab for every idea that comes along in your mind, you will spread yourself thin mentally, and experience utter frustration over feeling like a failure at never getting traction in any of your ideas. One of the challenges that I think many young people suffer from, is the fact they have lived through the growth of the dot com age of technology, where many bright, and not so bright, people in their early to mid-twenties, hit it huge with some type of technology development. Because of that and being told their entire life that they were as good as the best on the team, without any proof in their performance or earning those accolades, they have looked for the easy route to the good life, believing that they deserved it without hard work and persistence.

I'm here to tell you that 99.9% of people don't achieve greatness and the quality of life that they want, without hard work and paying close attention to the four Pillars and Characteristics in the *Path to the Ultimate Life* visual. If you are going to achieve success with your goals in life, it is important that you follow the path that I have laid out throughout this book, to discover the things that I have shared in this book, like your purpose, passion, priorities, and principles. These will help to keep you focused on the prize of life that you desire. The more you run from one idea to the next, the more you will be like a ball in a pinball machine, bouncing all over the place until one day you land in the hole. A few key questions to be asking yourself, in order to stay focused are:

- What am I good at?
- What are my strengths?
- What do I want to achieve?
- What do I like doing?
- What people do I want to help?

Asking these questions will help you to define what you would like to do in life. As you determine where you want to go, with your end game in mind, stay focused on that goal. As we talked in the chapter on threats, you don't let anything deter you from that goal. If it's important enough for you, and where you want to go in life, nothing should get in the way of it.

With that being said, I want to step back a moment and warn you to not let a goal become an idol in your life, to the point where you rule out the most important people around you, because of your pursuit of it. It happens every day. This is where your priorities are connected to your pursuit. If your family is your most important priority, then you don't become obsessed by working late due to your goal. Doing this means that you have elevated your work life as your number one priority, and you had committed in your plan to make your family your number one priority. Remember, financial security is a big deal for a family, but quality time is an even bigger deal. You need to find that balance.

If you are a college student and you want to find that first nice entry-level job, then you can't let the distractions on campus and potential relationships get in the way. That's not to say that you don't have fun in college. Live it up but make your studies your top priority. You will be glad you did when you are in your post college interviews, and the HR Director or President of the company asks you, "So what was your GPA?" What you say next will determine whether your interview goes any further. If finding a great offer out of college is not your goal, and you just want to have a great time in school and get a degree, with say, a 2.2 GPA, then go for it, and do it with all your might. However, hear me on this: You have just selected the long route to a great paying job. Employers look at your GPA, and say to themselves, "They had all the time in the world to work hard and study, and they didn't make the grades. What makes me think that they will work hard here at our company?" Once an employer is asking those questions, your interview is over. Your GPA is the measurement of your work ethic in college and shows an employer whether or not you are a hard worker.

Let me take a quick, little side tangent for college students, on the topic of relationships. I'm all for you going out with people in college. Have a blast. Get to know tons of people. However, when it comes to dating, I'm an advocate of not committing to a serious one-on-one relationship in college, for a couple of very specific reasons.

First, you will miss out on so much of the college experience. There is so much that goes on in college, that having an exclusive relationship will hold you back from experiencing. You will stop going to many exciting college events, because you will begin to separate yourself, staying at your place, hanging out together, thinking that the world now ends with the both of you. I'm here to tell you, that the world outside on your college campus is passing you by. College is the time to build your network of people around you. Get out and be a part of extra curricular activities, because one day in the future, those people that you meet are going to be Presidents of companies, Vice Presidents of departments, and influential people in the economy of your life. Once you leave college, all of those people will eventually be in a great place in life, and the one thing that will get you in the door to see them is that you are alumni, a fraternity brother, a sorority sister, or you have some other common bond that you were able to establish in college. When you pick one person in college that you choose to exclusively hang out with, you put yourself at a personal and professional disadvantage for the future.

Another big reason for this mindset, is that everyone you meet in college, is going to mature into different people over the next eight-to-ten years after graduation. Many of them will mature into someone who you wouldn't even give the time of day to, had you known how they were going to mature. I encourage all college students to make college your playground, to learn about yourself and others. Then use that experience and knowledge once you graduate, to find the person that you want to spend the rest of your life with. I've seen so many young people, who were great students in the classroom, but had a horrible work ethic in the workplace. The bad time to find this out, is a year into your marriage, because you dated early, got engaged your senior year, and married right out college.

Take your time. There is nothing wrong with waiting and enjoying life in college; learning who you are and letting the one you might want to build a life with time to grow up, so you get a sense of what you're getting into. The bottom line is: the emotional ups and downs of a young relationship can be a huge threat to you achieving your goals and the ultimate life you want in college. Make a wise choice.

Now for all of you out of college, the same holds true in running your business, having a successful marriage, moving up your career ladder, and in just "doing life." If you look at a glass as the amount of energy and time that you have to give to everything that you are going to commit to in daily life, you only have so much to give. Once your glass is full, it's full. If your glass begins to run over because of overcommitting, then everything inside the glass will start to run out also, and you will have a mess everywhere. You will begin to feel overburdened, overworked, and burnt out. You've become distracted from your purpose, you've lost your passion, your priorities are out of order, and you stopped having the "party" that refreshes your "glass of energy", because there isn't any room or time to enjoy it. You have lost your focus. That is why it is so important to narrow your focus on the things that are the most important to you and dominate that space.

Guard the amount of energy, emotions, and time that you commit to, so that you don't become average at anything. Commit to being GREAT at a few things. Whatever and whomever you commit to, you want to do it AWESOMELY! If you continually pull off awesome for people, Your Dash will be fulfilling, and your obituary will never suck.

APPLICATION TO MAXIMIZING YOUR DASH

What distractions keep you from being able to focus on your purpose?

What are the top three things that you need to rule out of your life, in order to get focused on your life?

In the area of choices, money, people, or time, which ones do you feel that you need to refocus on, in order to achieve your goals in life?

What would you like to be great at?

ACTION STEPS TO MAXIMIZING YOUR DASH

Write down three things you are going to rule out of your life, in order to help you bring clarity and focus to your goals.

Buy a written planner, or use the one on your mobile device, to start writing down the things that you need to do daily, to narrow your focus and achieve your goals.

Ask a close friend, who has a very organized life, to chat with you about how they stay focused on their goals?

CHAPTER 26

THE THREE QUESTIONS

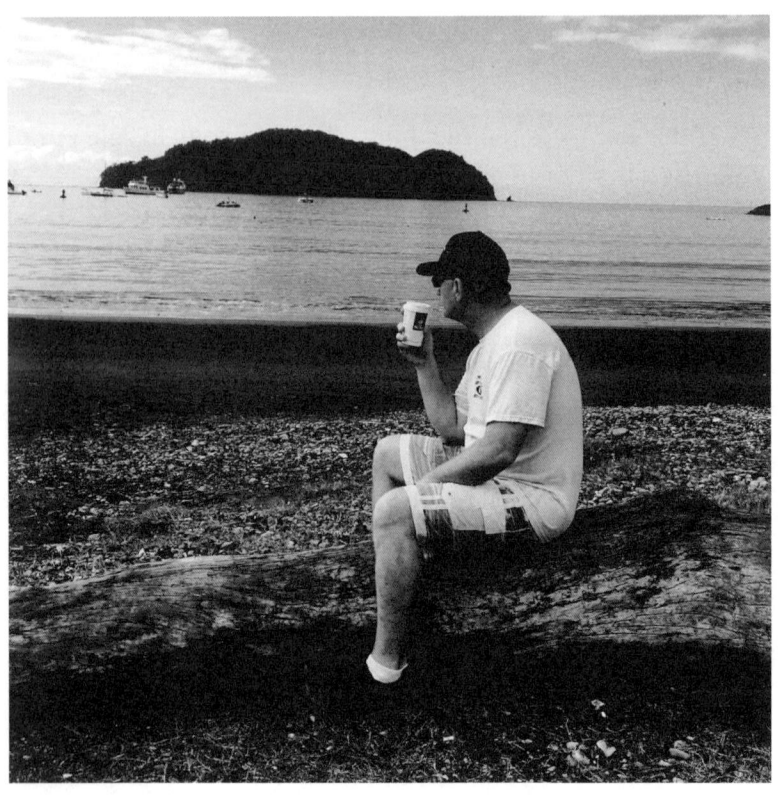

"Failure to learn the lessons of your mistakes, will allow you to keep making the same mistake over and over. Never be afraid to ask the right questions about your life."

With every plan in life, whether personal or professional, there are three questions that you must ask of yourself on a consistent basis. These three questions ensure you are on target to your goals, as close to the time frame that you wanted, and expose the gaps in your progress so you can make some immediate changes and you don't get sidetracked and off course.

It is important that you ask these questions about each area of the *Path to the Ultimate Life* visual. If you are to make positive changes towards your goals and purpose in life, then you will need to fine-tune, and make some big and some small changes in some, or all eight of the areas of this visual.

It is important that you ask the following three questions in the following intervals, but first consider the following to ensure success:

• Before you pursue your plan, make sure you start with good execution.

• Quarterly, in the first year, ensure that you make good progress.

• Annually, make adjustments given the changes that will occur (or have occurred) in life and your surrounding environment.

• The three questions that you need to ask in each area are:

• What am I CURRENTLY doing that I need to do differently?

• What am I NOT doing that I need to start doing?

• What am I doing that I need to STOP, because it isn't relevant?

I've put my *Path to the Ultimate Life* visual on the next page, along with the key areas that you will need to think through, as well as, the three questions for each part of the visual. This is a chapter about self-reflection and thinking through your life. You can choose to take the time to work through this in depth, and then read the last chapter, or read through the last chapter, and then come back to it.

This entire book has been helping you to think through

the key areas of your life leading up to this moment, when you will put the pieces of your life puzzle together.

Take time to analyze each area, and either write your responses in this book, or if there isn't enough room, write up a document that you can keep on your mobile device, so you can refer to it at anytime. I prefer that you write it in a document that you can refer to on your mobile device. It's your life plan. It's worth having with you at all times.

Good luck with your life analysis.

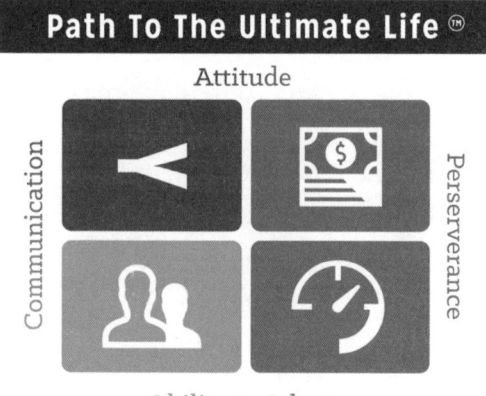

YOUR ACTION PLAN TO MAXIMIZING YOUR DASH

What is your PURPOSE in life?

What is your PASSION in life?

What are six core PRINCIPLES that you are going to live by?

1)

2)

3)

4)

5)

6)

Describe the key characteristics of the type of PEOPLE that you want to surround yourself with?

1)

2)

3)

4)

5)

6)

What organizations, or networks of people, must you become involved with in order to meet these types of people?

1)

2)

3)

4)

5)

Put the following PRIORITIES in the order that you want to live by? Add others in the extra space if you have any. If some don't apply to your life, mark NA on them. They may apply at some point in your future.

- Wife
- Other Family
- Work
- Education
- Personal Fulfillment

- Volunteering (church/nonprofit work)
- Children
- Friends
- Faith or Spiritual Beliefs
- Personal Health

What three things in your PAST must you forgive, accept, or let go of in order for you to embrace all that the future has for you?

1)

2)

3)

What is your "PARTY" that you are going to put on your schedule at least once a week, so you can consistently refresh your energy and passion in life?

GOALS (make one for each for next 12 months)

CAREER:

RELATIONSHIPS:

FINANCES:

HEALTH:

CHOICES I MAKE:

What am I doing now that I need to do differently?

What am I not doing that I need to start doing?

What am I doing that I need to stop because it's no lon-ger relevant?

HOW I INVEST MY TIME:

What am I doing now that I need to do differently?

What am I not doing that I need to start doing?

What am I doing that I need to stop doing because it's no longer relevant?

HOW I SPEND MY MONEY:

What am I doing now that I need to do differently?

What am I not doing that I need to start doing?

What am I doing that I need to stop because it's no longer relevant?

PEOPLE I'M SURROUNDED WITH:

What am I doing now that I need to do differently?

What am I not doing that I need to start doing?

What am I doing that I need to stop because it's no longer relevant?

POSITIVE ATTITUDE:

What am I doing now that I need to do differently?

What am I not doing that I need to start doing?

What am I doing that I need to stop because it's no longer relevant?

COMMUNICATION SKILLS:

What am I doing now that I need to do differently?

What am I not doing that I need to start doing?

What am I doing that I need to stop because it's no longer relevant?

ABILITY TO ADAPT:

What am I doing now that I need to do differently?

What am I not doing that I need to start doing?

What am I doing that I need to stop because it's no longer relevant?

PERSEVERANCE:

What am I doing now that I need to do differently?

What am I not doing that I need to start doing?

What am I doing that I need to stop because it's no longer relevant?

CHAPTER 27

YOU CAN'T ESCAPE YOUR LEGACY

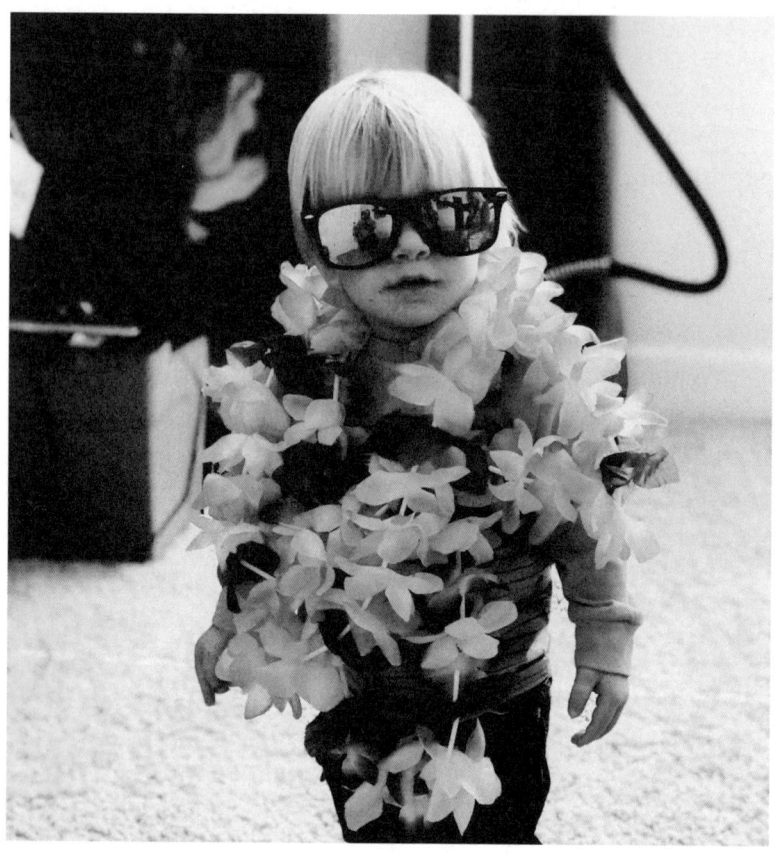

"Your legacy will live on for generations. Will it be good or bad? You get to choose."

Wow! I can't believe that our time is coming to a close. I can't believe that we have spent so much time together over the last twenty-six chapters, working through every aspect of what seeking the ultimate life can be for you and making sure your obituary won't suck. It's hard to bring things to a close. I've shared with you so many of my stories, challenges, and the things that I have learned in life. You have looked deep into your life, shared the things that you want to change about your life, and built a plan to succeed…which is awesome. I appreciate you being open and honest with yourself. You have established a path to achieve the things that you want in life, that are going to have a lasting impact on your life, as well as, all of those around you, including your family, kids, and friends.

Whether you like it or not, like Your Dash, you will also have a legacy. No one gets to escape it. Your legacy is going to either be good or bad. The image that you leave behind, is either good or bad. The memories that you leave behind with your kids, grandkids, family, and close friends, are either good or bad. Your legacy is what you leave behind. Some people reading this book, only need to make slight changes in order to leave behind a good legacy for their children and grandchildren. Others, need to make big changes in their lives to break the generational curse of struggle that has plagued their life. I recall an interview that I heard once, from a well-known boxer, who was asked by the reporter, "You are vicious in the ring, like a raging tiger who is angry. Where does that emotion come from?" He replied, "I hated my father and the way he treated me as I grew up. Every time I get into the ring, it's my time to get even with him." As a father, I feel for him, because he has this huge hole in his soul, and a longing for his parent to love him. He wants to carry on his father's legacy, but he can't, because of the amount of pain that goes with it. Many people carry that same pain, from someone in our life who we deeply cared about. For many, it is their parents. If you are on the path of leaving a painful legacy behind, and want to change, YOU CAN! Hope is in your plan that you have thought through with this book.

No matter what your age, your children will one day carry your legacy with them into the future. Is your legacy one that can empower and build their life? …Or it is going to be a legacy that they will struggle with for years? I'm asking these questions, because I want you to think about your legacy as you begin to pursue your goals and enhancing your quality of life.

Winston Churchill once said, "We make a living by what we get. We make a life by what we give." I encourage you to be a giver of life, not a taker. If you give all around you, life will come to you in ways that you never thought possible, because giving is like a magnet…it draws people to you.

I feel that in life, people are always looking for H.O.P.E. all around them. To me, H.O.P.E. is a great acronym for people that portray a:

- **H**ell of an attitude
- **O**ptimism
- **P**assion
- **E**nergy

Seek to be a person who brings a positive attitude, optimism, passion, and energy to those you come in contact with each day. Remember, anything worth doing, is worth doing with all your might. Keep a copy of the ***Path to the Ultimate Life*** visual on your mobile device. Focus on the four Pillars in your decision-making process. Improve on the four Characteristics needed, in order to do the four Pillars with excellence. Pay attention to your threats. Work your life plan. Expand your network of people continually. Keep your legacy in mind as you flow through life. Most importantly, rate your Personal GDP every quarter and work on the areas you are weakest in. As your Personal GDP rises, you are living life to your fullest and making sure your legacy and your obituary won't suck.

Thank you for sharing your time with me in this incredible journey. As you look at what tomorrow will bring, GO BIG, GO BOLD, AND GO NOW! You will never regret making the decision to improve your life and chase your dreams.

ACKNOWLEDGMENTS

First, I would like to say Thank you to all of all my industry friends across the country, in the Florida Society of Association Executives, American Society of Association Executives, and the Council of Manufacturing Associations. You know who you are. Business as well as life is boring if you aren't creating friends in the industry you work in. The relationships, friendships, and life long memories you have helped me create have provided the platform for which much of this book is about. Thank you for giving me life each year.

I would like to thank my parents Jeanette and Charlie who have sowed so much into my life. Dad, thank you for sharing how a man can care, have compassion and under-standing. Thank you for being willing to be firm in your words and discipline to keep me focused on making good choices. Mom, thank you for giving me the drive to be suc-cessful and a natural born energy to enjoy life every day. I'm proud to be your son and call you my mom and dad.

To my kids and their spouses, I have so much to say and so little room. Thomas and Kristin, Brittany and Joseph, Kristen and Garrett... You continue to be an inspiration to me as young adults and now parents. Your love and compas-sion for people and direction you have chosen for your life is exciting and shows me there is great hope for the future in your generation. Thank you for being such awesome chil-dren, young adults, spouses, and SSD's (super step daugh-ters)! And remember... "Make Good Choices!"

To the most important person in my life, my wife DeAnna, I would like to say THANK YOU for being such an amazing support and encourager in my life. I knew on our first date (Feb. 12, 2011) that you were they one. You are amazing to wake up to, live life with and go to sleep with every day. You have been the number one inspiration of this book and thank you for pushing me to write my second book. I love you and our adventures forever.

Lastly, I would like to thank God for giving me the inspiration and words to write this book. Thank you for having the strength above mine to pull off such amazing things during my life. Thank you for always being there for me to handle the smallest of details and make the biggest miracles happen. Without you, I'm just another guy. With you, I have tapped into strength above my own to help change people's lives each day.

AUTHOR BIO

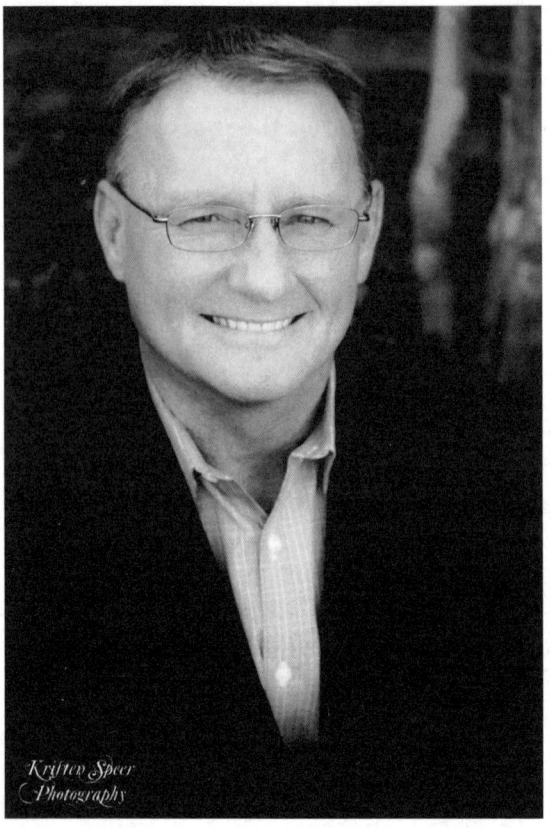

Tom Morrison is a seasoned 20-year veteran in executive management and life coaching. He is an author, nationally known speaker, and CEO of Tom Morrison and Associates. As a Certified Life Coach, Tom's passion has always been to help people see that no matter what your circumstances are in life, if you want something more, you can achieve it.